IN-SOURCED

CONTEMPLATIONS FOR CONSCIOUS & MIRACULOUS LIVING

IN-SOURCED

CONTEMPLATIONS FOR CONSCIOUS & MIRACULOUS LIVING

HELEN CONNOLLY

BALBOA
PRESS
A DIVISION OF HAY HOUSE

Copyright © 2012 Helen Connolly

All rights reserved. No part of this book may be used or reproduced by any means, graphic, electronic, or mechanical, including photocopying, recording, taping or by any information storage retrieval system without the written permission of the publisher except in the case of brief quotations embodied in critical articles and reviews.

ISBN: 978-1-4525-6355-8 (sc)
ISBN: 978-1-4525-6356-5 (e)

Library of Congress Control Number: 2012921775

Balboa Press books may be ordered through booksellers or by contacting:

Balboa Press
A Division of Hay House
1663 Liberty Drive
Bloomington, IN 47403
www.balboapress.com
1-(877) 407-4847

Because of the dynamic nature of the Internet, any web addresses or links contained in this book may have changed since publication and may no longer be valid. The views expressed in this work are solely those of the author and do not necessarily reflect the views of the publisher, and the publisher hereby disclaims any responsibility for them.

The author of this book does not dispense medical advice or prescribe the use of any technique as a form of treatment for physical, emotional, or medical problems without the advice of a physician, either directly or indirectly. The intent of the author is only to offer information of a general nature to help you in your quest for emotional and spiritual well-being. In the event you use any of the information in this book for yourself, which is your constitutional right, the author and the publisher assume no responsibility for your actions.

Cover Photograph of Helen and Eugene, from 'In-Sourcing and the Upward Facing Dog' (page 78) taken by Robyn Connolly, 2009.

Printed in the United States of America

Balboa Press rev. date: 12/03/2012

To the divine beloved source in all

In memory of Eugene
(July 14, 1999–June 21, 2012)

Contents

Foreword . . . . *xi*
Preface . . . . *xv*
Acknowledgments . . . . *xix*
Thirty Seconds of Friction 1
Beach Glass 5
Five Quotes That Get Me Through a Tough Day 7
A Perspective on Perspectives: Enlightening Lessons from a Washed-up Fish 15
Contemplation on "If" 19
Consider the Apples 23
It's All for Good —Robyn's Version 29
It's All for Good —Helen's Version 33
The Groundhog and the Potato Vine 37
Yes, and ... Life as an Improv Skit 41
The Scaredy Caterpillar 49
When I Forget to Focus on Gratitude 53
Watching Channel One 55
Weather Patterns 59
Flags and Original Innocence 63
Talking Trees 67
Ask and You Shall Receive…Just Be Wakeful How You Ask! . . 71
What Works, What Doesn't and Do We Really Know Which Is Which? 75

Isabel and the Light	79
In Memoriam	83
Awareness That Space Is God	87
In-Sourcing and the Upward Facing Dog	89
People of the World Untie	97
A Blissful Christmas	101
What Is God Worth to You?	103
A Life In Clothes: Living the Material Myth	107
Adapt, Adjust, Accommodate	111
Decisions, Decisions	115
Communion, Poetry of the New	119
My Evening with Marilyn	123
I Am Here Now	129
Do You Know Where You're Going?	131
The Fog and the Sun	135
I Am No-Body, I Am Soul	139
Spiders and Webs	143
Identity Loss and Reward	147
Just Another Day in Paradise	151
The Liberation of Loss	155
Just Be	159
House Beautiful	161
Afterword	165
About the Author	167
Resources	169

Education is an admirable thing, but it is well to remember from time to time that nothing worth knowing can be taught.

—Oscar Wilde

Foreword

Many people are trudging along a hot, rugged path in the desert toward the Promised Land. As deprivation and hardships increase, faith lags, and some even begin to doubt the existence of the heavenly destination.

A helicopter arrives and a few are lifted straightaway to an indescribably beautiful place, where they quickly forget the painful challenges left behind.

They cannot stay in this glorious state, however, and are taken back to the barren wilderness. But for these fortunate ones, everything has changed. They continue trekking with the group but with a quiet strength and contentment, for now they no longer just believe in the Promised Land; they *know it exists*. They have been there!

This is a description of people who have had a near-death experience. On returning to life, everything has changed for them. They have no fear of death, they have a deep sense of purpose, and they see with an expanded vision.

Helen Connolly has been to the Promised Land. She doesn't *believe* it exists; she *knows* it exists. She has been there!

On February 29, 2008, at her Toronto-area home, Helen had a near-death experience. We may never know everything that was gestating in the interim, but exactly nine months later, on November 26, 2008, Helen was at the Oberoi Hotel in Mumbai, India, and survived the infamous terrorist attacks. Two beloved companions at her same dining table were shot and killed while Helen sustained only a minor gunshot wound. She shares those remarkable stories here, along with many others—all bearing the priceless gift of knowing clearly how to apply each as a lesson.

Helen and I first met in 1993 when I conducted a spiritual workshop in Ontario. As we became acquainted, I learned more about her. She was beautiful, young, and married, with two wonderful, healthy children and a lovely home. Some might say she had everything. But while Helen was thankful for the many blessings in her life, it was as though she had heard an inner call and was restless to find the unknown "something else" that summoned her.

Since then, in her quest for self-realization, she has endured many personal and spiritual transformations and diligently, faithfully prepared herself as she felt directed to do from time to time. She has conducted yoga and meditation classes for fifteen years, to the benefit of her many grateful students. Now Helen's loving service expands yet again with the contribution of this marvelous book. She writes here in a very practical and down-to-earth way of her moment-to-moment journey through everyday life with the inestimable blessing of inner spiritual guidance. She is walking along the path with fellow travelers but has a deep peace and clarity that comes from having experienced the all-fulfilling bliss and love that are present beyond the veil of ordinary human experience.

As I finished reading this manuscript, I felt greatly uplifted by the high consciousness and spiritual energy embodied in it. Helen's metaphors resonate on many levels. Metaphor is the language of the soul, and the soul is speaking here. I feel honored and blessed to know Helen and to recommend this book to all her readers. As Helen states over and over again, this book was written not by her but through her.

Namaste,
Christina Thomas-Fraser, MA
Encinitas, California
September 2012

Preface

> First you were fine. Then you were de-fined. Through yoga (union with the Divine) you are re-fined.
> —Sri Swami Satchidanandaji Maharaj

Why am I here? What's life for exactly? Was there a memo dispatched that I didn't receive or perhaps a practical joke that I wasn't in on? Such were the thoughts of my youth. I am the youngest of seven children, and my father always told me the midwife at the hospital placed me in his arms and said, "Here's someone to look after you in your old age." He was close to fifty when I was born, which was already considered pretty old back then. I grew up with that affirmation, but that never quite felt like my purpose.

The idea of heaven and hell fascinated and scared me, as did the doctrines of the Catholic Church in which I was raised, but they also didn't make any logical sense to my innocent child's mind. Why would God create so many different types of people if so many of them (us) were destined for eternal damnation? As a child, I never found joy in the destruction of beauty. Why would God? I also wondered how God could have made us in his own image if we were miserable sinners. It seemed like a pretty mean thing to do, and surely God wasn't mean! And who made God anyway? I felt a love for God in my heart, but the teachings just didn't add up in my head. Something was missing here.

As for life, if you played by the generally accepted rules and won all the prizes; the friends, the education, the career, the money, the guy or the girl, the house and kids, the power, the status, what then? Was that 'it'? Was there a point I was missing in all of this? I never got satisfactory answers, but it didn't seem to bother anybody else, so I learned to keep my mouth more or less shut, like a good little girl but I kept reading and wondering.

Initiation in Transcendental Meditation at the age of eighteen set the stage for new possibilities and definite stress reduction for a few years until the practicalities of a full-time external life focus took over.

My parents died quite suddenly when I was in my early thirties followed shortly thereafter by an ectopic pregnancy and miscarriage. This inspired a whole new and more intense line of questioning on the purpose of life and death, fuelled by intense grief and depression, which thankfully led me to wonderful teachers and profound realizations that changed my outlook and thus my experience of life.

The line that separates the lack of awareness of my unconscious self from my present experience of life is like the chrysalis that surrounds the caterpillar. It provided a container for transformation to occur as I moved from a dense, fragmented life experience to a more subtle, whole, blissful and playful consciousness. Awareness is the magic wand that created such a transformation.

In this book, I am passing on that honed understanding or more wakeful perspective to you. When we *really* know better, *in our cells* and not just conceptually, we do better. When we do better, we are better, and so is the whole universe. After all, the universe is made up of each and every one of us, and our emissions are powerful, so we need to take responsibility for what we emit.

The first step is to realize that the source of all the answers you seek is found within. In a world that outsources everything, constantly seeking gratification, stimulation, and validation from an external focus to fill "the gap" in life, please know this: *You are a self-contained unit of the divine.* Outside mentors and resources like this one may point the way and inspire, yet you are the destination you seek. To discover the truth of who you are and for lasting fulfillment in life *In-Source* your awareness through meditation and contemplation; don't put all your eggs in the outsourcing basket. It's fragile and by itself it never fulfills for long. Every single thing in form began its existence in formlessness. Meditation is the gateway to such an infinite resource and blissful experience of your true nature.

This book is my invitation to you to be your part, to be who you *truly* are, to drop your illusory stories, and play with me in original innocence.

> Life is simple. Minds make it complex.
> —Master Charles Cannon

You will find that many of these contemplations have similar themes that are told in different ways to help us remember the universal wisdom and the truth of who we are. Instead of reading the book from start to finish in one sitting, take your time with each chapter. Let it settle into you like a stone dropped in a pond. Let it send ripples of recognition to all of your cells.

Trust and watch the response of body, mind, and spirit. You may experience doubt, skepticism, and resistance as the ego tries to retain its claim on you. That's okay. Just trust and watch.

You may experience a sense of upliftment, delight and yes, recognition of truth from a place eternal and deep within yourself. That's okay. Just trust and watch.

> What you are looking for is what is looking.
> —St. Francis of Assisi

> In our obsession with original sin we do often forget original innocence. Don't let that happen to you.
> —Pope Innocent III to St. Francis in *Brother Sun, Sister Moon*

Acknowledgments

Ask and you shall receive, we are told. In an effort to find peace with the process of life I brought my questions, fears, and frustrations into consciousness and boldly asked for divine guidance.

I asked and I listened. Answers flowed from within, just as the questions once did, from periods spent in deep meditation and contemplation, assisted over many years by the study of spiritual material and the mentorship and energetic transmission of an exalted list of enlightening human beings.

During one summer break, some of my yoga and meditation students asked me to keep in touch with them via e-mail, so I sent weekly notes about what was in-sourced through my meditations and contemplations. This book is the result, along with many new additions.

Thank you to my students for inspiring this communication. Thank you for further requesting them in book form. Thank you for sharing yourselves with me and helping us to grow together.

Thank you to all the blessed ones, living and passed on, who have shared their bliss with me in order of their appearance in my life: Christina Thomas-Fraser, who first lit my lamp and flooded the darkness with her light and continues to do so, and her husband, Campbell Fraser, Paramahansa Yogananda, Babaji, Suresh Goswamy, Sri Swami Satchidanandaji Maharaj, Swami Karunananda, Swami Asokananda, Dr. Amrita McLanahan and all the staff at Satchidananda Ashram Yogaville, Swami Jyotirmayananda, Ammaji, Master Charles Cannon, Catherine Marks and all the staff at Synchronicity Foundation for Modern Spirituality, Alan, Kia and Naomi Scherr, Sai Maa, Osho, Sri Sathya Sai Baba, Shirdi Sai Baba, Jaimangal Krishnanand, Sri Satua Baba, and other sages and saints too numerous to mention, but you know who you are. I am profoundly grateful. I delight in your virtue!

Thank you to Deirdre Kavanagh for caring enough to be the light bearer; to Dr. Stephen McLaren for useful instructions on playing well in the sand box; to Blaine Watson for charting the course, to Isabel Caceres for so many things and to Lorraine Gilks for her encouragement, editing suggestions, friendship, and support.

Thank you to Dan Goldstein and Tom Tollenaere for gracious permission to reprint their work here regarding improvisational acting. My gratitude goes too, to all others whose work is quoted here and to those who inspired these contemplations.

Thank you to Audrey, Brandon, Cara and all the staff at Balboa Press for shaping this book into the form you see before you.

Thank you to my husband, Dan and my children Robyn and John, and of course Eugene, for your love and support, and for providing me with many opportunities to learn and expand my consciousness. Thanks too for accompanying me during the whole sometimes uncomfortable and challenging evolutionary process and for permitting me to use our stories for the benefit of others.

Thank you, dear readers, for permitting me to share my bliss with you. The bubbling fountain needs somewhere to flow. The fountain is now flowing in your direction. Joy in receiving blessings is doubled when we are permitted to share that joy with others. Your presence multiplies my bliss.

And finally, thank you to the one ecstatic divine love which exists blissfully within and around us all, continually raining love upon us, if we take the time to see.

Thirty Seconds of Friction

I SAW A FILM TRAILER FOR the film *Barney's Version*[1] on TV in which Barney tells someone he's getting married. When he is asked to whom, before he can respond, a female voice cuts in, with the camera focusing on her very pregnant belly, and says flippantly, "To me. Prince Charming Bomb here knocked me up by way of a magical thirty seconds of friction," or something like that.

Crude though it may have been, that comment really resonated with me. I guess in the most basic sense, we were all created from thirty seconds of friction. Imagine that. The entire population of the world and everything that's in existence was created from friction! Every tree and blade of grass is the result of roots and shoots in friction with the soil; every coastline was carved out through friction with the waves of the ocean; warm campfires are the result of friction between two sticks.

---

1 | *Barney's Version*, directed by Richard J. Lewis (Toronto, Ontario: Serendipity Point Films, 2010).

Friction[2] is the necessary precursor to new life—to transformation. The recent transformation in the Middle East is the result of friction between the energy of the masses and the energy of the powers that be.

Yet friction in our own lives gets such a bad rap, including friction in our marriages, in our families, in our workplaces, in our neighborhoods, between our hearts and minds, etc.

Friction itself is neutral, just as a knife can be used to spread butter or inflict suffering. It depends on how we view it and use it. It's an indicator light telling us that something is happening.

Let's reframe all the frictional events in our lives, shall we? Instead of resisting the friction, let's ask ourselves: What new life—what transformation—is being made possible by this friction? Who do I choose to be in relation to it? Do I choose to be strong and fearless or resistant and fearful? Is it possible in that moment to be loving, inclusive, and allowing? Do I choose to remain in witness consciousness,[3] observing what's going on and my response to it, or do I choose to react from unconscious ego? Am I angry and upset or crystal clear in communication? Do I remain in integrity with what is or indulge in fragmented, illusory stories through which I view the present moment? And most importantly, do I choose to be for giving or for taking?

The options are many, and the freedom of choice is ours. Everything is appropriate depending upon where we are in terms of conscious awareness.

Whether you abide by the big bang theory, which some say created the universe, or believe that God/source made the world (presumably out of God/source material, because what else existed?), a wonderful

---

2 | Maharishi Mahesh Yogi's response to disciples who came to him in a deep state of friction was, "Ah, something good is happening here!" (Courtesy of Alan Scherr.)

3 | Witness consciousness is the balance point of detached neutrality between the positive and negative polarities of life. For more on this see Resources for Synchronicity Foundation information.

example of infinite possibility has been set in place through friction. How would life be for us if we chose to view friction in that light and live up to its example?

Be the light that you are.

Beach Glass

I was thinking about beach glass after a meditation recently. The image just popped into my head—the smooth, colorful pieces you find washed up on the shore. Have you ever found two identical pieces of beach glass? Each one is unique, beautiful, and refined by its communion with water and sand. It has a preciousness that you can't buy mass produced in a supermarket.

It's a good metaphor for each one of us. As we pass through life, we are sculpted by our interactions with everything and everyone. When we place our lives in the hands of our divine selves, we are smoothed and polished even more. Swami Satchidananda[4] said we are like stones in a bag that the divine shakes and shakes (there's that friction again!), rubbing away the roughness to polish us and make us shine. Note that he did not say it is to make us all the same but to make us shine!

The temptation of enculturation is to conform, like bottles neatly stacked in the grocery aisle or liquor store, to fit in and do what everyone else does. But why should we? The fact is, we didn't arrive

---

4 | Sri Swami Satchidananda, founder of Satchidananda Ashram, Yogaville, Virginia. See Resources for further information.

all together in a delivery truck, fresh off an assembly line, and it's also likely that most of us will leave one by one. Why are we here if not to be the fullest expression of ourselves? That includes our innate divinity, which is life itself. It's the first to enter and the first to leave when we drop the physical form. It's the home base of uniqueness, and from lifetime to lifetime, it is our individual consciousness—a spark of all that is. You *are* that!

Of course, it occurs to me that beach glass most likely started out its journey as a generic bottle or jar, on a shelf somewhere before it broke free! Is there any area of life where you unconsciously conform to something that is not conducive to being the fullest expression of your divine self?

Often in order to survive a situation that is not in alignment with the essence of who we are, we self-medicate with dependencies on food, alcohol, sex, drugs (prescription or otherwise), work/busyness, money, power, status, television, sports, etc. Yet these same things keep our bodies, minds, and emotions distracted (as in off track) from experiencing our own *swadharma* or unique life purpose. In our efforts to avoid our illusory fear of emptiness or loneliness, we also block the exquisiteness of the self, which, if faced, would lead to true bliss.

We are powerful beyond our imaginations. We are complete and whole beyond all our perceived needs and habits. Dare to stand back from the habitual mind, take a seat in the heart, and look at this life *you* are living. Dare to break free in some way today! Start on any level—physical, mental, or emotional. It doesn't have to be something huge. In doing, in doing, it is done! Remember, it starts with a conscious thought or intention that is aligned with *the heart* of the heart. Let your beach glass shine as only it is meant to do!

Thought > Word > Action> Habit > Character > Destiny
How will you shape your destiny today?

Five Quotes That Get Me Through a Tough Day

If you do what you've always done, you'll get what you've always gotten.
—Christina Thomas-Fraser[5]

Would you rather be right or happy?
—Christina Thomas-Fraser

I am here. It is now.
—Master Charles Cannon[6]

---

5 | Christina Thomas-Fraser is the founder of The Inner Light Institute and is an internationally published author and teacher. See www.innerlightinstitute.com.
6 | Master Charles Cannon is the spiritual director of Synchronicity Foundation for Modern Spirituality. See www.synchronicity.org.

> Your suffering will be in direct proportion to your resistance of what is.
> —Master Charles Cannon

> Don't think. Look.
> —Jaimangal Krishnanand[7]

A story: We are in our *tenth* week of a six-week basement renovation that started at the beginning of May. We added a yoga studio renovation to the job because the workmen were already here and their craftsmanship seemed ideal for what needed to be updated in the studio. We figured the work there could be done while we were away on vacation.

But the cottage we rented for the month of July is being occupied only by my son at the moment. It's still a fantasy for Dan and me. Delays, setbacks, and *friction* of all kinds are to be expected in this line of work. We're used to that and can roll with what is, keeping our eyes focused with gratitude on the transformation. However, this week something so unexpected happened and brought up such processing[8] for me that I had to resort to some of my favorite quotes, listed above, to help realign my energy and bring me back to a state of balance. It was so illuminating to my attachments and judgments, enculturation and fears, and it caught me by surprise for what, on the surface, seemed like such a little thing. I thought you might enjoy hearing about it. (My apologies if you'd rather not. Feel free to just skip ahead to the next contemplation!)

---

7 | Jai Krishnanand is a homeopathic doctor and teacher of metaphysical healing. See Resources for further information.

8 | Processing refers to a state of upheaval where we get stuck in our enculturated data from the past or our future oriented stories and forget the truth of who we are. In the process we miss the experience of being eternal and timeless presence in the now. Witnessing our process and including it allows us to clear old data, increase our awareness and evolve.

We had just dealt with a major issue of re-laying the new bathroom floor due to an error the tiler made in matching the color tones. Thankfully he came through for us and corrected the mistake, though it meant we had to put off our vacation to oversee the remedial work to completion. I assumed the contractor was now aware of the standard of workmanship required (mistake number one; never assume anything!), and I was grateful when he said he'd have his men in to lay the wood floor in the studio hall and powder room on the weekend we had to stay home so it would be in place before the painter arrived a few days later.

My intuition raised a red flag when the man who showed up to do the work was not the same carpenter who had done such a good job in the basement, but the contractor assured me he was good. (Mistake number two; do not ignore those intuitive red flags!) The second red flag went up when I asked what kind of threshold he'd brought to finish the edge between wood and carpet, and he disinterestedly responded that it wasn't his job and the carpet guy would figure that out.

Okay! *Say no more, Helen*, I thought to myself. *You've already blasted the tiler this week.* I decided to stay out of it and see what emerged. Well, what emerged was the worst handyman special imaginable, complete with all the rubble of the old flooring tossed onto the yoga studio floor and industrial glue wiped onto the landscaping rocks outside the door in the sanctuary garden. When he called me down to inspect the new floor he had glued down to the sub-floor, I thought it must be a cruel joke—except that I wanted to cry, not laugh!

My thoughts and emotions went something like this:

1. Denial: This can't be happening. He's kidding, right?

2. Fear: Oh my God, I've just ruined the beautiful studio.

3. Guilt: Sacrilege ... This is a desecration of sacred space. How could I have let this unconscious person in here?

4. Fear and Guilt Combined: I can't possibly let this floor stay. It's a terrible first impression of a supposedly wakeful space. I hate it. The students will hate it! But what about saving the environment if I have to rip it up?

5. Anger and Judgment: What kind of idiot was I to believe the contractor when he said he was good? What kind of contractor would tell me (or think to himself) that he was good? What kind of person would lay a floor like this and think it was good? Etc.

Do you see how the mind works to create story, fantasy, frenzy, and nightmare that take one out of conscious presence? After weeks of renovation challenges, I was finally in high process. This exceeded my quota of tolerance, or as Master Charles might say, "My peak management skills were exceeded." That caused me to lose my usual peace and balance; a learning curve was sprung upon me!

I put calls in to my husband and the contractor. I was so upset that I picked up a novel and started reading to distract myself from what I was powerless to deal with in that moment. (This is a method of bringing positive dominance to a negative dominant energetic state, thus aiding in regaining a position of balance in favor of a stormy emotional state. By removing oneself from the situation physically or mentally, one can create perspective and regroup.) Still, moments later, my husband had to remind me to breathe when he returned my call! Isn't that funny? Why is it that when consciousness plays hide and seek, it often takes its coping mechanisms with it? In truth, we cut the connection to such wisdom with our imbalanced state. It is always there for us.

Here's what I (re)learned:

a. Attachments steal your happiness. The closer you are to something, the larger it looks and the blinder you can be to the attachment. I felt that the studio was my gift to God. I was devastated that it had been disrespected. My daughter reminded me that I am my gift to God, not the building. Big lesson! Aren't kids great teachers? (Note to self: I must have had good karma to have attracted such wise kids into my life!)

b. Judgments, like expectations, steal your happiness. This is not to condone bad workmanship. It is merely not to confuse the deed and the doer. Judgments close the heart, which cuts us off from the divine flow of awareness, so we suffer more than those we judge. As the truth of who we are is oneness, that judgment sticks to us. Indifference (neutrality) or compassion is key here to reopen the heart. If they knew better, they would do better. When I know better, I do better. It works both ways and also allows us to be kinder to ourselves when we mess up.

c. Enculturation runs deep into the subconscious and can be a reflexive action until awareness brings transformation. I grew up in a perfectionistic household. Mistakes were not easily tolerated. Judgment of the mistake maker was swift. This is part of my journey—to discard what is not the finest expression of self. (This is my smoothing of the beach glass!) It is enough to include this facet of my personality and transcend through awareness without adding to the illusion by judging myself harshly for judging others!

d. If I always react as I was programmed by my enculturation, I will get what I've always gotten, which is a vicious circle, if you stop and think about it. When awareness dawns, it is necessary to consciously choose differently. The question is, "Who do I choose to be in relation to this situation?"

e. Sometimes in the heat of the moment, I unconsciously choose to be "right" when I'd really rather be happy. I forfeit peace of mind for anger, frustration, or desire for things to be other than they are. Thus my suffering is in direct proportion to my resistance of what is.

f. "I am here. It is now." If I can be precisely aware of *exactly* what is taking place, devoid of the dramatic story that is being scripted by my mind from past enculturation and future fears, I will be present to the moment and what it presents. Just being ... and breathing ... and being ... and breathing ...

g. "Don't think. Look." If I come from emptiness, I remain balanced. If I come from thoughts, opinions and stories, I become unbalanced and I'm not in a position to deal with what is in an effective manner. Simply looking reveals this fact: The floor is not okay. It needs to be replaced. End of story. No drama. Calmness reigns. No big deal! This factual communication was relayed through my husband, whose state of mind was more detached in that moment. (It was not his place of work or sacred space, after all!) I surrender it all to the universe for the highest good of all concerned. And somewhere in heaven, God is laughing!

PS: My son thoroughly enjoyed his bonus of a week's solitude at the beach cottage and had things nicely set up when we got there.

PPS: The end results of the renovation of the basement and studio are really beautiful in appearance and peaceful in vibration, and I learned so much along the way, for which I am grateful!

See how things work? It's all for good!

A Perspective on Perspectives: Enlightening Lessons from a Washed-up Fish

I was lying on my belly on a blanket in the sand just outside the cottage when my son came up from the beach with a tennis ball and a hurling stick. As he passed by me on his way up the steps to the deck, he said, "There's a big dead fish on the beach, and the ball hit it."

I asked where the fish was, and from his position on the deck he said, "Over there where all the birds are. They're pecking at it."

I turned my head to look but could see no birds. I was about to ask what birds but decided against it, rising instead to walk in the direction he was pointing, trusting that there were birds there, even if they were invisible to me at the moment. As I followed the path for a few steps through the undulating dunes, I saw the tops of feathery heads appearing. After a few steps more, the white and speckled heads of a small flock of seagulls came into view. Sure enough, there in their midst was what was left of a large fish, about two and a half

IN-SOURCED

feet long, mouth open wide, scales glistening in the sun as the skin rippled loosely in the gentle waves of the shore's edge.

How beautiful, I thought. The whole cycle of life and death was at my feet, thanks to whatever calamity caused this fish to die. I had the privilege of examining it up close. Its skin was floating gracefully like an ethereal gown with huge couture sequins. What had fleshed out this dress was now being recycled into nourishment for the gulls, leaving a beautiful, strong skeleton and skull. There was no bad smell. Nature had provided a most efficient clean-up crew.

"Isn't it gross?" commented my son when I returned to the cottage.

"It's the same skin and the same bone that it had when it was alive. The difference is that the life force has left it. It's clear that you value the life force more than the physical form," I said.

"Isn't that interesting?" I continued. "You instinctively value what is essentially invisible and recoil from what is most visible, unless it's being served for dinner with French fries, of course! Then the reverse applies!"

This little interaction was an enlightening experience on several levels regarding perspective, and I thank my son for being the catalyst for these lessons.

First, and most obviously, our experience of something is dependent upon what we bring to it. The gulls' gain was my son's disdain and my science and metaphysics lesson. Here was positive dominance, negative dominance, and witness consciousness in action all at once[9].

Second and very epiphanous for me was the, "Birds—what birds?" element of the story. Something that was patently clear to

---

9 | From the Oneness of Source Consciousness comes the Relative Field of form, comprising a positive polarity, a negative polarity and the space in between. See *The Synchronicity Experience*, pages 6 and 7 for further information. Master Charles Cannon. *The Synchronicity Experience*, Nellysford, VA. Synchronicity Foundation International, 2002.

my son was completely beyond my vision; how often I have become frustrated in life when something that is obvious to me is not at all apparent to another! Have you ever had that experience when dealing with a child, a teen, a spouse, a store clerk, or dare I say a contractor?

The simple question is how do we know where we are standing and where they are standing? It may look like we are occupying the same space and time, but are we really? There are planes upon planes within the physical realm alone, and just a few steps can make a big difference to what's immediately available and apparent to us.

But what about planes of consciousness, from the densest to the most subtle, from the most ignorant to the most illumined? So I ask again, how do we know where we are standing? What lifetimes and experiences in number and quality have shaped our awareness and those of the other?

How do we create a scale of acceptability when everyone is a unique facet of the divine on his or her own evolutionary journey? Ultimately we all attain liberation from illusion. My responsibility is to my own adventure and my own choices, constantly chipping away all that is not reality and universal truth. I have no business judging anyone else's choices or expression of source.

Third, this story brought the guru to mind. The word *guru* refers to darkness and light. The guru is one who leads us from the darkness of ignorance and illusion to the light of truth about who we are and what life is. He/she/it is the one up on the deck with the high vantage point, pointing the way to the light. We may be lying on our bellies in the sand, saying, "Light—what light?" We have to trust that the teacher/guide can see what we, at this moment, cannot. We have to trust enough to walk in the direction of the guru's guidance until his or her vision becomes clear in our sight line and we can see for ourselves.

IN-SOURCED

When that happens, there are no more questions. Relative perspectives merge into a unified experience, the great oneness.

Aha! Now we get it! Yes!

And I thought I was just going outside to sunbathe ...

Contemplation on "If"

"If"[10] by Rudyard Kipling is a beautiful summary of the teachings of yoga and the Bhagavad Gita[11] that culminate in self-mastery and enlightening states of being. It touches on witness consciousness, detachment, oneness with all, balance and wholeness, faith in the higher self, forgiveness, patience, humility, looking beyond external differences to be one with the essence beneath, integrity ... I could go on. See for yourself and enjoy!

If

If you can keep your head when all about you
Are losing theirs and blaming it on you;
If you can trust yourself when all men doubt you,
But make allowance for their doubting too;

---

10 | "If—", Rudyard Kipling, Poetry Foundation, last accessed October 25, 2012, http://www.poetryfoundation.org/poem/175772#poem.
11 | Sri Swami Satchidananda. *The Living Gita, The Complete Bhagavad Gita*, 4:19-23. Buckingham, Virginia. Integral® Yoga Publications. 1988. Fourth printing 2000.

IN-SOURCED

If you can wait and not be tired by waiting,
Or, being lied about, don't deal in lies,
Or, being hated, don't give way to hating,
And yet don't look too good, nor talk too wise;
If you can dream—and not make dreams your master;
If you can think—and not make thoughts your aim;
If you can meet with triumph and disaster
And treat those two impostors just the same;
If you can bear to hear the truth you've spoken
Twisted by knaves to make a trap for fools,
Or watch the things you gave your life to broken,
And stoop and build 'em up with worn out tools;
If you can make one heap of all your winnings
And risk it on one turn of pitch-and-toss,
And lose, and start again at your beginnings
And never breathe a word about your loss;
If you can force your heart and nerve and sinew
To serve your turn long after they are gone,
And so hold on when there is nothing in you
Except the Will which says to them: "Hold on";
If you can talk with crowds and keep your virtue,
Or walk with kings—nor lose the common touch;
If neither foes nor loving friends can hurt you;
If all men count with you, but none too much;
If you can fill the unforgiving minute
With sixty seconds' worth of distance run—

Yours is the Earth and everything that's in it,
And—which is more—you'll be a Man my son!

Master Charles suggests, "If life is a game, why not play it *masterfully?*" For me it's really the *only* game worth the effort in the big picture. It offers the greatest fulfillment.

Would you agree? What step can you take toward true self-empowerment and self-mastery today?

∞

Consider the Apples

This little story for children of all ages came to me in meditation, inspired, no doubt, by one of my favorite movies, *Brother Sun, Sister Moon*,[12] which deals with the life story of St. Francis of Assisi. In his meeting with Pope Innocent III, St. Francis is inspired to quote from Matthew 6.

This biblical version of what he had to say is from the King James Bible online, Matthew 6:27-34. (It sounds better in the movie!)

[13]And why take ye thought for raiment? Consider the lilies of the field, how they grow; they toil not, neither do they spin:

And yet I say unto you, that even Solomon in all his glory was not arrayed like one of these.

---

12 | *Brother Sun, Sister Moon*, directed by Franco Zeffirelli (Italy: Euro International Film, 1972).
13 | Matthew Chapter 6:28-34. The Official King James Bible Online. Authorized Version (KJV), accessed October 25, 2012 http://www.kingjamesbibleonline.org/book.php?book=Matthew&chapter=6&verse=28-34

Wherefore, if God [our true nature] so clothe the grass of the field, which to day is, and to morrow is cast into the oven shall he not much more clothe you, O ye of little faith?

Therefore take no thought, saying, What shall we eat? Or What shall we drink? Or Wherewithal shall we be clothed?

(For after all these things do the Gentiles [the spiritually unawakened] seek:) for your heavenly Father [Source consciousness] knoweth that ye have need of all these things.

But seek ye first the kingdom of God, [the stillness of the divine self within] and his righteousness; and all these things shall be added unto you.

Take therefore no thought for the morrow: for the morrow shall take thought of the things of itself.

Mom sliced an apple into pieces. Jake reached for a wedge. As he bit thoughtfully into the juicy flesh, he asked, "Mom, who makes apples?"

"Apples come from apple trees," said Mom. "So I guess the tree makes them."

"How does the tree know how to make them?"

"That's a good question, Jake. I don't know how the tree knows. Why don't we go to Grandpa's backyard and you can ask the tree yourself?"

Hand in hand they strolled down the road to Grandpa's garden and stopped to admire the beautiful apple trees, laden with ripening fruit. Jake ran up to one of the trees and hugged it.

"Thank you for my apple, Ms. Tree. It was delicious. My mom says all our apples come from you, and I would like to know how you make them. Won't you tell me pleeease?"

"Well, Jake, it's true that apples come from me. But I don't make them," the tree replied.

"You don't? Then who does?"

"I can't say. All I know is that the other trees and I just stand here every day with our roots snuggled into the yummy brown earth. It feels good just being with Earth, and somehow that feeling nourishes me. I do love my friend the earth. Perhaps she makes the apples.

"Almost every day, another friend, Sun, shines on me, warming me, and that makes me want to stretch my branches toward her light. I do nothing but hang out with Earth and Sun, playing and dancing with our friend, Breeze, and it feels so good that my happiness just explodes into blossoms. I stand here and watch it happen. Perhaps Sun makes the apples.

"Some days Rain comes and bathes me in her cooling showers and quenches my thirst. It's a party for Earth and me. We get all cleaned up and drink our fill. We don't have to work or do anything. We just are, yet our being together seems to make my flowers grow bigger, and I look and feel *so* pretty! When I'm at my prettiest, the bees come and tickle and dance their way through my petals. We sway and flutter in the breeze, along with the other apple trees. They visit lots of flowers, and some of my dusty pollen decorates them as they buzz and play. They love the nectar in my flowers and sip it to their hearts' delight. They like to party! Perhaps they make the apples, though I don't know how or when, as they just seem to enjoy themselves!

"After my flowers drop away, tiny apples start to appear. It's the most amazing thing, Jake. Little apples just start to grow on me. They get bigger and bigger and change color from green to a beautiful golden red. I watch in wonder as some of my little ones are picked, some fall away, and some that grow way, way high even hold onto me for most of the winter, dusted in snow like Christmas ornaments.

"And still I do only what comes naturally. I just am. Each year a new crop of my family comes and goes.

"I don't mind how my beautiful babies live their lives. That's not my business. They have their own adventures. They get to experience each moment joyfully, with whatever and whoever shows up to share life with them, just like I do here, with my friends. I know that doesn't answer your question, so perhaps you should ask my friends if they make the apples."

Jake thanked Ms. Tree and spoke to the earth. "Earth, do you make the apples that grow on Ms. Tree's branches?"

"Oh no," said Earth. "I just lie here in her warm embrace and am happy to be with her. She is so peaceful and strong. She holds me in place so I don't blow away when Breeze gets too playful. I feel good and send her love and gratitude for being my friend and always being there for me."

Jake thanked Earth, looked up to the warm sunshine, and asked, "Sunshine, do you make the apples on Ms. Tree's branches?"

"Oh no, I don't think so," said Sunshine. "I just shine because that's my nature. It's who I am. I like to shine on her so I can see her better. It fills me with happiness to soak up her prettiness. My warmth seems to bring a smile to her flowers and fruit. But make apples? That sounds like work. Go ask the clouds who drop the rain showers. Maybe they know about work."

Jake saw a puffy white cloud near the sun and asked, "Mr. Cloud, do your showers make Ms. Tree's apples?"

"'Fraid not," said the cloud. "Not my department. I just float about soaking up water, and when I get really full, I fall out of the sky and visit my friends below. They love my visits. It seems to refresh them. If you listen closely, you can hear them sing and giggle as I tap and touch them with my raindrops. But make apples? No sir. I don't know anything about that. Isn't making things hard work? I just go with the flow, man! You've got the wrong guy!"

Just then a breeze fluttered through the clothes drying on Grandma's clothesline. It looked more like a chorus line as colorful socks and stockings kicked up their heels.

"Hey, Breeze, wait up," called Jake. "I'm trying to find out who the apple maker is. Is it you?"

"Who, me? No kid, I'm just passin' through. Love 'em and leave 'em—that's my motto. I don't stay around long enough to make anything," said Breeze.

Well, that just left the bees and the trees. Jake swirled around to face the other trees.

"Don't even ask," they called out as one. "The exact same thing happens to us. We have no idea how. But here are a few bees. Ask them."

They shook their branches to scatter the bees that were investigating some apples that had fallen on the ground.

"Hi, bees, do I thank you for the apples? Did you make them?" asked a bewildered Jake.

"No way," they buzzed. "But they sure do taste good," they said as they hovered over the bruised apples.

Now Jake was really confused. Here were these beautiful and delicious apples that somehow got made. It must be very hard work to make something so wonderful, and yet, as far as he could tell, no one made them at all. They just seemed to come from a lot of good friends loving each other and having fun together. Everyone seemed to have a unique nature, and the sharing of those natures created magical things, like apples, to appear … It was a "mys-tree" all right!

Jake ran to his mom and reached up for a big hug.

"Thanks, Mom, for bringing me to Grandpa's. I love being with you. Maybe that's what makes me grow too!"

The life force that is our true nature flows through everything and is the author and co-creator of existence. Loving ourselves keeps the floodgates of creativity wide open and playful. Sharing that love with others makes the apples of our lives grow sweet!

It's All for Good
—Robyn's Version

When my kids were little, I used to read stories to them from a book entitled *Enlightening Tales*[14] as told by Sri Swami Satchidananda. Now that they are both adults, it still delights me when they remember stories from that book at just the right moment.

One of those stories was called "It's All for Good" and teaches how seemingly adverse circumstances are still orchestrated by God or source for the highest good of all. We just have to trust and watch. After the following event took place, my daughter called me and said, "Guess what happened, Mom … It really *is* all for good."

My daughter's work frequently necessitates that she spend several hours a day outdoors downtown regardless of the weather. One rainy spring morning she donned her heavy rain boots, tossed her new Converse sneakers into a tote bag for indoor wear, and grabbed a cab

---

14 | Sri Swami Satchidananda. *Enlightening Tales*. Buckingham, Virginia: Integral Yoga® Publications, 1996, Page 25.

to work. She usually walked or took the streetcar and subway, but she indulged in the luxury of a taxi because she was running late. She'd received a petty cash reimbursement from her office the night before in the form of $50 bills. She'd already mentioned at the office that she'd prefer to be repaid for her expenses in small bills, as cafés, cabbies, and bus drivers were not enthusiastic about taking $50 for small expenses. Now here she was stuck with nothing smaller with which to pay the driver. (It's a good complaint, I know, but you know what I mean.) She hoped he'd take it.

She hoped in vain. With too many fake fifties floating around and too great a safety risk involved in carrying a lot of cash in case he was robbed, the taxi driver was apologetic but unmoving. Society's flaws were not working in her favor as she rushed to work. She dug her wallet out of her bag to pay by debit card. Now she was really going to be late. She punched in her PIN, took her card back, and raced out of the cab. Only when she got to her office did she realize her forgetfulness.

"Oh no, I left my shoes in the cab!"

She pulled out the debit card receipt for contact information and called the cab company to explain her dilemma. They were not very hopeful.

"Did you pay by cash?" asked the dispatcher.

"No, I paid by debit," Robyn replied.

"In that case," said the dispatcher, "let me pass you over to customer service and maybe they can radio all of the drivers."

Robyn explained her story again to the nice girl on the line. She added, "They're brand new shoes. I haven't even worn them yet!"

"Oh honey," said the girl, "I hope the next customer doesn't wear the same size shoe as you! Did you get the driver's name and license number?"

"No, I looked at his plate, but I don't remember his name."

"Do you remember what the driver looked like?" asked the young woman at the call center.

"Yes. Would it help if I told you he was young, like twenty something?"

"Was he kind of cute looking?" asked the girl, suddenly more interested.

"Yes, actually he was."

Eager now to help, the service agent said, "I think I know who it is. Leave it with me and I'll get back to you."

Sure enough, soon after, Robyn received a call from the good-looking cab driver to say he had her shoes. Within minutes he drove to meet her, and she was delightedly reunited with her new cherry red sneakers.

The probability of my daughter being reunited with her shoes in a major, busy city was slim, but she kept the faith that all would unfold as it should. If she had had smaller bills, she would have paid cash. She would not have had a debit receipt with the name of the cab company, would not have been put through to customer service to the nice young girl who seemed to have a crush on a handsome young cab driver, and most likely would not have seen her brand-new shoes again! Ah, source, you've just got to love its sense of play and possibly its match-making techniques too!

As a postscript to this article, over the years, Robyn has left her scarf on the streetcar and a pair of gloves on the bus since then, and miraculously she has gotten them all back through the wakefulness and kindness of her fellow man. Along with the return of her scattered wardrobe comes the gift of her renewed faith in humanity! It's all for good!

It's All for Good
—Helen's Version

I HAVE HAD SO MANY EXAMPLES of this realization in my life that I could fill another book, but for illustration purposes, I'll share with you one of the first heart-stopping examples of this that I experienced.

When my kids were little (and I was just new to the spiritual path), we decided to take a trip to visit some old Irish friends in Newport, Rhode Island. It's a popular vacation spot in the summer, and not having accommodations booked months in advance, we were lucky to find a vacancy in a settlement of very humble cabins a short walk from the beach. The furniture was old and shabby, the wooden bed creaked with every twist and turn, and it smelled a bit musty, but it functioned and we were happy to have a place to stay.

One day as I walked to the beach, I noticed a stunningly beautiful Victorian mansion down a quiet roadway off the main beach road. Its fish-scale shingles were painted a glistening white and wraparound verandahs were dotted with pink and purple petunias overflowing from pale wooden planters. A big old tree—a chestnut, I think it was—stood in the middle of a sweeping lawn, and from it hung a rope swing. A rabbit nervously munched on grass. I stopped to gaze at this idyllic sight and thought to myself, *Imagine staying there.* I felt grateful just for the privilege of enjoying the view and continued my walk to the beach, not saying a word to anyone about this lovely home or thinking anymore about it.

Now let's fast forward to the next year. We called our friend in January to ask him to find a place for us to stay during the coming summer. He rented a nice basement apartment very close to the beach. Great! We anticipated our vacation with glee. However, just a few weeks before we were destined to depart for Newport, he called to say that the landlord found a tenant to rent the space for the whole summer and had canceled our reservation!

"What? Can he do that?"

Well, apparently so, because he did. Our friend told us not to worry and he would try his best to find somewhere else, but at this late stage it was hard to be optimistic.

About a week later, he called to say he had found us another place. We asked where, but he said it was difficult to explain the location so he suggested we meet at a spot in town and he would drive ahead of us there in his car. At that point we would have agreed to anything just to enjoy our vacation by the ocean.

Twelve or so hours of driving later, we met him in town. He drove ahead of us onto the beach road and then made a left turn onto a quiet road. My heart skipped a beat in my chest. I think it actually stopped for a moment or two! *Oh my God, he has led us to the glistening Victorian mansion with the wraparound verandahs and the pink and purple petunias! How can this be happening?* I thought.

Well, it turned out that the mansion was divided into a few apartments. His friend lived in the one on the main floor with the verandahs, and it was he who had planted the colorful flowers that cascaded from their pots. Because he had a son who visited with him on weekends, he had hung the swing on the tree! It just so happened that he had to go out of town on business for two weeks when our vacation was planned and offered to rent his home to us! My mind struggled to make sense of all of the ramifications of this. Just how many strings did the universe need to pull to orchestrate that home run?

To this day it still blows my mind! Needless to say, we had a wonderful vacation. Not only was it a lovely home, garden, and location, but the bookshelves were stocked with spiritual reading material. I was in heaven! When we weren't on the nearby beach, the kids had a fun time with the rabbits and the neighbor's cat, the lawns to roll on, and the delightful swing.

What had shaped up to be a disastrous vacation turned out to be one of the most memorable ever!

From this experience I learned that if I can continue to go with the flow when things are not going my way, who knows where it will take me. Perhaps the universe has a better idea. I trust and watch that it's all for good!

The Groundhog and the Potato Vine

Once upon a time there was a lady who loved the divine. By divine I mean the source or creator, maintainer, and destroyer of all creation—the big kahuna, the answerer of all questions, the solver of all problems, the unconditionally loving one of which we are all a part. Some people call this one God, Brahman, or the Absolute. She liked to call it Baba. It had a nice affectionate ring to it, slipped easily off the tongue and into the heart, and was as good as any other label. It meant Father in Sanskrit.

Everything she did, she did for Baba (or at least as often as she remembered). Before she would eat a bite of food, she would say, "All for you, Baba." When she cleaned the house, washed the laundry, or shopped for groceries, she would silently affirm, "All for you, Baba," in thanks for all Baba had given her.

It was natural for her to whisper, "All for you, Baba," as she tucked annuals into her patio planters at the beginning of the warm spring weather. Impatiens, ivy, geraniums, and two kinds of potato vine were all lovingly offered to the divine.

IN-SOURCED

Soon after planting, watering, and fertilizing, she noticed some leaves missing from the vibrant green vines. The next day they were even barer, nibbled to the stalks. Drastic measures were called for. She reached into her spice drawer for the cayenne pepper and dusted all the leaves with the hot pepper. That should dissuade any feasters from destroying her lovely plants. But no, the next day even more of the vines had been eaten, and as she stood in the backyard talking to her husband, she saw the culprit approach and begin to munch.

Jumping up and down and waving her arms, she yelled, "Shoo, get away from my potato vines. Shoo, shoo!" As the guilty groundhog ran away, she explained her frustration to her husband about how the spice did not act as a deterrent.

"Maybe he likes a spicy salad," joked her husband. "Didn't you say they were all for Baba? Don't you remember the story in *Enlightening Tales*[15] about God coming as a dog to enjoy a feast offered by a devotee?"

Just like that, the light of awareness dawned. "Oh my God," she said. "You mean that perhaps that has been Baba coming daily to enjoy my offering and I have shooed him away out of the mistaken idea that the plants were mine!

"Forgive me, Baba," she said. "They are all yours. If you wish to eat them, please do so. I was being unconscious in thinking they were mine. Thank you for coming to accept my offering. I have learned my lesson."

After that, she stopped worrying about the plants and the predator. She stopped putting cayenne pepper on the leaves. The funny thing was that the potato vines were never eaten again, and they grew lush and strong and radiant. They filled up the planters. They cascaded down the sides and spilled along the ground. They

---

15 | Sri Swami Satchidananda. *Enlightening Tales*. Buckingham, Virginia: Integral Yoga® Publications, 1996, Page 100.

grew with such abundance that thoughts of Jack and the beanstalk came to mind.

As the lady and her husband marveled at the incredibly rich and lush display of chartreuse green and burgundy black vines, the lady, only half-jokingly, asked, "What else can we give to Baba?"

The moral of this tale is that what you resist persists. What you can include seems to melt away and transform into something greater than you could ever imagine. And somehow the experience leaves you wiser and stronger in your transcendence.

If you think about it, perhaps this is Baba's way of saying, "All for you, my beloved one, all for you."

Yes, and ...
Life as an Improv Skit

I READ AN INTERVIEW IN THE *Toronto Star* with Lisa Kudrow[16] recently in which she said she'd been studying improvisational acting. Ms. Kudrow described a widely used practice in improvisational acting, sometimes referred to as "Yes, and..." to ensure that the scene flowed, where you replied to whatever the other actor had to say with this response and then went on to build on what he or she had said. If you blocked or denied what had already been said, you would trash the whole scene and everybody would lose.

What a brilliant tool to apply in life too, I thought, stating the obvious to my satisfied self! I decided to investigate more and was surprised by how yogic the rules were. Why I should be surprised I don't know, as the art of improvisation merely imitates life, so it's logical that what creates a happy, relaxed, and harmonious experience on stage might also work in the muppet show we call life.

---

16 | Phoebe from the TV show *Friends*.

In addition to the number-one rule mentioned above and with respect to the contributors of the websites listed in the footnote,[17] here's what I discovered online, complete with my own yogic perspective:

1. **Take care of yourself.**

    - Improv says if you take care of yourself, you will appear at ease. This in turn puts the audience at ease. If you stand on stage doing nothing and looking confused, everyone has a negative and uncomfortable experience. Therefore, look after your own needs with a fulfilling activity.

    - Yogic perspective says we are all one. If, on some level, you are in pain, I see it and feel it. Therefore it's necessary and not selfish for you to care for your own needs. The perfect yogic act is one that benefits at least one person and harms no one, *including oneself.* Taking care of yourself brings you to a state of balance. The resultant abundance of love and contented fulfillment will naturally spill over on everyone. This makes everybody happy. Happiness is as contagious as misery, so take care of yourself. Far from being selfish, it is your contribution to the world. Neglect of oneself is no more virtuous than neglect of a plant, animal, or child in your care! Everything together makes up the universal garden.

---

17 | "5 Basic Improv Rules," Improv Encyclopedia, last accessed October 12, 2012, improvencyclopedia.org/references//5_Basic_Improv_Rules.html. "First 10 Rules of Improv," Improv Encyclopedia, last accessed October 12, 2012, improvencyclopedia.org/references//David_Alger%60s_First_10_Rules_of_Improv.html "How to Be a Better Improviser," Dan Goldstein, last accessed October 10, 2012, www.dangoldstein.com/howtoimprovise.html.

2. **Go line for line**

    + Improv rules tell us that if each actor bases his or her response upon the last thing the other character said, then a good show is almost guaranteed.

    + Yogic perspective says: Be an aware, listening consciousness, focused and present in the now. Listen to the words and the spaces between the words, the action and the inaction, knowing that source communicates subtly, and if we are absent or distracted, we may miss something precious. This presence creates a harmonious and unified experience instead of warring partners bent upon destruction or control.

3. **Accept silence and being self-conscious**

    + Improv says it's okay to be self-conscious. It's okay to be silent. Don't be afraid to respond without words. Being self-conscious doesn't mean we have to work to entertain or try to please. We can be conscious of what's going on with us and allow communication to be natural, authentic, and multidimensional.

    + Yogic perspective: Sathya Sai Baba[18] said not to speak unless what you have to say improves upon the silence! Sometimes silence tells us everything we need to know, so don't miss the opportunity to let it speak. Listening to your self-consciousness allows you to step outside it (into the witnessing audience, if you will) and let its story run without

---

18 | Sri Sathya Sai Baba (1926–2011), Indian Guru, mystic, educator, and philanthropist. For more information see Resources.

getting involved in it emotionally or judgmentally. Such awareness allows for evolution to take place.

4. **Enter and exit with purpose.**

    - Yogic perspective: You are here for a purpose. Make use of the opportunity to evolve your conscious awareness and wholeness while in physical form. Be ready to exit when the time is right, feeling complete with your "live performance for a limited time only." Resist the impulse to live on automatic pilot.

5. **"What makes today special?" is a fine question to ask yourself.**

    - Improv says to think about a scene as a day unlike any other day. When it feels like something big is going to happen ... do it.

    - Yogic perspective: Each moment is new, unique, and unrepeatable. Be aware. Be alive. Experience the extraordinary in the ordinary, the divine in the everyday. Go with the flow of what's happening, embrace, include, complete, and transcend whatever it is.

6. **Sooner is better than later. Do it now.**

    - The rules of improvisation state that when an opportunity for action comes up—do it! Don't speak about it, don't lead up to it, and don't put it off.

    - Yogic translation: In life when we are totally present, we have more power, focus, and clarity. Procrastination creates stagnation of one's energy.

Talking dissipates energy. Instead of talking our intentions and dreams away, we can pour that energy into taking the necessary action to make it a reality.

7. **Have fun and relax.**

    - Improvencyclopedia.org tells us that improvisation should be fun. An audience loves to watch someone having fun. By letting go of fear of failure, we commit more, focus more, and become more fully.

    - Yogic perspective: This principle is very effective in everyday life. Worth adequacy issues such as, "Am I good enough? Will I screw up? Will they hate me? Will they fire me? Should I do this instead of that?" arise in everyone. These future-based and fear-based thoughts and emotions consume a great deal of energy and focus that could be used more productively by focusing on the moment and situation at hand. Trust that you are in the right place at the right time doing what you are supposed to be doing and that life is unfolding as it should and let go of the fear. Fear cannot be experienced simultaneously with love. Love is our true nature. We have to drop fear to fully experience our own power and bliss. Relax, have fun, and choose to love what is.

8. **Change, change, change**

- David Alger's *First Ten Rules of Improv* [19] says, "Improv is about character change. The characters in a scene must experience some type of change for the scene to be interesting. Characters need to go on journeys, be altered by revelations, experience the ramifications of their choices and be moved by emotional moments."

- Yogic perspective: This is what is referred to as the evolutionary journey of source, constantly re-creating itself for the delight of itself through each one of us. Conscious choices, openness to learning from challenges and experiences, and evolving to more than we have ever been as we relinquish our ego's attachments to stories and outcomes—this keeps us open to the gradual (or sometimes sudden) realization of the eternal and infinite self within us and around us.

Here are a few more universal commandments of improvisation graciously provided by the websites listed:

- Give and take.

- Yogic perspective: Treat the other as you would wish to be treated.

- Work to the top of your intelligence.

- Yogic perspective: Be wakeful and aware.

---

19 | "First 10 Rules of Improv," Improv Encyclopedia, last accessed October 12, 2012, improvencyclopedia.org/references//David_Alger%60s_First_10_Rules_of_Improv.html

- Thou shalt not shine above thy teammates. (S)he who tries to be clever is not, while (s)he who is clever doesn't try.

- Yogic perspective: Ego tries to shine brighter than others. The enlightening ones shine without trying. Their light radiates naturally from their inner stillness and state of allowing.

- When thy faith is low, thy spirit weak, thy good fortune strained, and thy team losing, be comforted and smile, because it just doesn't matter.

- Yogic perspective: We are infinite and eternal and it's just a play of consciousness unfolding in the now, meaning only as much or as little as we choose to interpret with the limited mind.

- Tried. Failed. No matter. Try again. Fail Again. Fail better.
  —Samuel Beckett

- Yogic perspective: This is the evolutionary journey from fragmentation to wholeness, gradually learning from and moving from our stories and excuses to a life of integrity.

- Dan Goldstein's website leaves us with a quote by Mick Napier, the award-winning director at The Second City:

"Improvisation is the art of being completely okay with not knowing what the f*** you're doing."

IN-SOURCED

- Yogic perspective: The idea that we know what's happening next in life is just illusion. In fact, in the eternal now, next is an illusion. In the world of maya (illusion) we live with the principle of uncertainty and life and source as the ultimate mystery. So trust and watch the show. Stay tuned to see what happens next. Then choose to be okay with it (i.e., balanced, detached, and transcendent).

So, ladies and gentlemen, if I may have your attention please! In this improv skit known as life, all that we ask is that you relax and enjoy the show!

If you'd like to learn more, all improv information was excerpted with gratitude from the following websites:

- improvencyclopedia.org/references//5_Basic_Improv_Rules.html

- improvencyclopedia.org/references//David_Alger%60s_First_10_Rules_of_Improv.html

- www.dangoldstein.com/howtoimprovise.html

The Scaredy Caterpillar

How does a caterpillar feel when it emerges to find itself a butterfly?

I was watering the plants in the August heat when a butterfly fluttered over to check out what I was up to.

It inspected the freshly splashed leaves, having a sip, no doubt, as it hovered and bobbed about. It stayed long enough for me to consider how different its life must be now that it's no longer a caterpillar.

Just imagine for a moment—you are a multi-legged and multi-footed individual with a rather lumpy body that has brightly colored licks of yellow, white, and black.[20] Despite all those feet and legs, you plod along slowly, desperately afraid you'll fall off your platform and drop way down theeere! And all you want to do is eat. Eat, eat, eat—you literally eat the floor from under you (i.e., the milkweed leaf you were hatched onto) before moseying along over and doing the same to all the other leaves nearby.

---

20 | . "The King of Butterflies", Monarch Butterfly Website, last accessed October 25, 2012 monarch-butterfly.com.

IN-SOURCED

"I'm getting fat! Do I look fat?" you ask yourself. "I'm such a slob. Nothing interests me but food."

This goes on for about two weeks, which is a very long time in caterpillar life, at which time you find yourself at the bursting point and very tired indeed from all the energy consumed by endless munching.

"I'm a total failure," you say to yourself. "What have I got to show for myself except fat and fatigue?" You think you're going to fall apart from this seemingly pointless existence, and your horizontal stripes definitely do nothing to console you about the weight you've gained! So you do. You fall apart, sort of. Your exoskeleton splits and engulfs you in a kind of silky sleeping bag. You hang yourself from a leaf and give up. You feel like you've buried yourself alive, but you're too tired to care and you drift off into oblivion. So much for life!

Ten days or so pass. You've slept almost a whole other lifetime considering you spent only two weeks as a full time "cater-eater." Great! Now you've gone from obsessive eater to professional sleeper. Does nothing exciting ever happen in life, you wonder? Eat, sleep ... that's it? On top of all that, your sleeping quarters are decidedly cramped, you notice, as you wake up to find your silky chrysalis is hard and brittle. You can hardly move. You take a deep breath and try to stretch that lumpy body out to its full length. The chrysalis splits. You drop head first out of the bottom of it and hang onto the shell for dear life. But wait a minute! What's happening? Whose are these long, glamorous legs hanging onto the pupa?

"Where are my stumpy little legs?" you ask. "What's going on here?"

You take another deep breath and feel something rustle on your back. ("This is weird—really weird!") You feel your blood rushing to these really pretty pleated things on your back, and as you breathe in, they grow even bigger, stretching out like sails in the wind.

"Oh my goodness!" you exclaim. You try to stretch again, and they actually move. These gorgeous things move! *"I am making them move!"* In excitement, you shake them some more. There are four of them you notice, two up, two down and ... whoa! You have lift off. You're flying! And your body is now skinny and light as a feather! And your eyesight is so much better!

"Look at the view from up here! Who am I, and what just happened here? Was I abducted? Am I a caterpillar? I know for sure I was the last time I looked."

You look for a water droplet to see your reflection. Suddenly you are also thirsty from that mind-blowing float through the air. *"I can fly through the air ... I am floating through the air! How is this possible?"*

You spot a dew drop and lower yourself onto a broad green leaf. *"I can lower myself onto things just like that! Can you believe this?"*

You try to press your mouth to the water to drink, but you bump your ... "What the heck is this?" There is a great, coiled circle where your mouth used to be! "Get a load of this!" You draw your head back and stretch, and the coil unwinds into a super-duper straw. "Oh my goodness, I have my own straw! I can reach deep into flowers for the sweetest dew and nectar! What a gift. Who thought of this?" You feel like a queen!

You see a beautiful, angelic creature reflected in the droplet. It's an ethereal vision of orange and black and white, with a lithe black body and legs that go on forever. You move this way and that, and it mimics your every move.

"It's me! That angelic beauty is me! What did I do to deserve this? All I did was eat and sleep!"

Suddenly all of life is a party. Weeks go by as you flutter from flower to flower in the warm summer weather. You're feeling joyful and frisky and in the mood for love. You notice other creatures that look incredibly like you, and you dance through the air to get to know them better. They feel just like you do, incredulous at their good fortune and overflowing with joie de vivre. Love springs from such an abundance of good cheer. You feel fulfilled and content. All your desires have been met. Gratitude has been expressed. Love has been shared. Only one thing is left to complete your life experience and make your final contribution to all of existence. You find a milkweed leaf and lay some eggs.

And then you relinquish this beautiful body and its incredible life on this magical planet. It was a life that you thought was pointless and pathetic when you just looked at it phase by phase, but it looked remarkably different when you surrendered to the ebb and flow of the master plan of existence. You don't even know how many flowers, fruit, and people are thanking you for the gift and uplifting grace of *your* existence. Simply being yourself, including all changes and enjoying life harmoniously, was all that was necessary to bring joy, benefit, and transformation to yourself and others. You've had your time. Now it's the next generation's turn. You smile, say good-bye, and head back on home to the source point of creation, leaving just the body behind.

"Bodies are expendable," you say with a laugh. After all, you've gone through two in just seven or eight weeks. But you go on forever!

Life, with its journey of spiritual awakening, is like that!

(For the butterfly experts among you, this story refers to third-generation monarchs only.)

When I Forget to Focus on Gratitude

When I forget to focus on gratitude, I find I count my have-nots instead of my blessings. The have-nots grow so large under the microscope of my concentrated focus that all my blessings are obliterated from view.

In the undulation of positive and negative polarities, yesterday's cause for celebration becomes today's reason to suffer, as if the two experiences are entirely separate and disconnected, quite literally poles apart.

When I neglect to focus on gratitude, I neglect to see the common threads that link the two experiences. What is the commonality between such diversities?

First, the experiencer (i.e., my individuated consciousness) and second the co-creator of the experience, life force itself (i.e., source or universal consciousness).

When I forget to focus on gratitude, I forget that I, as individuated consciousness, am an integral part of universal consciousness, as is all and everything. I forget then that there is no difference between the experiencer and the experience, just as there is no difference between my inhalation and the air around me.

When I neglect to focus on gratitude, I lose my balance position that sits at the mid-point between feeling positive and negative, and with it, I lose my peace of mind. I careen over to the negative side of the scale and forfeit the grand vista of witness consciousness where both joy and suffering are entertaining episodes, enjoyed from my throne of peace and equanimity.

When I neglect to focus on gratitude, I forget the benevolent universe and decry my momentary fate. The universe, however, does not forget me, and neither does it forget that it is still creating the show and that my forgetfulness is part of the act. It's simply more entertaining and more dramatic for everyone that way.

At some point a critical mass of suffering and forgetfulness is reached, and the undulation begins again.

Suffering gives way to insight if we are open to its signs, and out of the depression the next wave rises.

Gratitude is remembered, blessings are counted, the heart expands, love is experienced and shared, and balance is regained until the whole process of hide and seek begins again.

Practice makes perfect. Challenges make for good practice, and so it goes and so it goes. We evolve with each step.

And in the process I learn that when I *remember* to focus on gratitude, life feels a whole lot better.

Watching Channel One

What if all we had to do was sit back and relax, find a comfortable position, and enjoy whatever appeared on the screen of our life?

What if there was no right way to react to whatever we witnessed and no wrong way either?

What if everything was appropriate and everything was educational, even if it appeared as comedy, tragedy, romance, or documentary? What if it was all entertaining and fascinating to behold, the same kind of present moment fascination a baby exhibits as it discovers its toes?

What if we evolved simply through our awareness and through our ability to be okay with whatever is going on in each moment, experiencing everything totally and completely? What if all we have to do is simply allow and include the show without judgment? What if we could let go of resistance to what is here and now?

"How is that possible?" you ask. "Surely as a sentient human being I'm going to have reactions and opinions. I have a voice. Am I not supposed to use it?"

IN-SOURCED

Well, yes and no. Yes, you are a human being with five senses and lots of karmic, cultural, and familial historical data that pulls the strings of those senses. But you are also so much more than that. I'm suggesting that you consider coming from the cutting edge of your discernment here rather than from the reflexive bottom rung of unconscious reaction, where it's automatic to shoot first and apologize after. As a purely sentient human being, you are on the surface of life, heaving yourself up and down with each passing drama, with every attraction and aversion, worrying and fretting, loving and hating, wanting and resisting. It's exhausting and without intermission because when we are not focused outwardly, judging every moment, we are focused inwardly, second-guessing or judging ourselves. Whew! What a chore. Do that for eighty-five years and see how fulfilled you feel!

How about switching from this multi-channel arena of dualistic experiences to Channel One?

What's Channel One? This is the channel that plays constantly behind all the other dramas on the screen. It was playing before all the other scripts of your life were written and acted out. It's also the one that will continue to play when all the other channels close down. It is the most inspiring, has no advertising, and will not stress you out. It's also very quiet. It transmits its wisdom without an outward sound. And the magical thing about watching Channel One is that when all the other programming is superimposed upon it, they appear most entertaining and not nearly as serious. They become more transparent, for once you become aware of Channel One shining through the other shows, it lets you see them for what they really are, like when you catch a glimpse of the puppet master behind the Punch and Judy show.

Will you have opinions and reactions? Possibly. Will they be implemented automatically? No. You will be empowered to choose your reaction to the experience you are having and to let your opinion be there without necessarily feeling the need to impose it. You will not be enslaved by your senses and your historical and "soulular" data. Or you may simply surprise yourself by having no reaction at all other than acceptance of what is, responding with a detached, "Is that so?"

When you are present to Channel One, the oneness at your very own core, the same oneness that is at the core of every other person, place, and thing that is manifested in form, you may find that preferences and opinions gradually fade away, so peaceful and fulfilled do you feel, so connected to the drumbeat of the universe that all seems in divine right order and nothing needs fixing, altering, or being in any way other than it presents itself in each moment. Then everything is orchestrated for the joy of it, according to the intuitive dictates of Channel One and not out of fear that all happiness would be lost without the multi-channel having its say.

How do I subscribe to this marvelous channel, you ask?

Meditate, meditate, meditate. It doesn't cost a dime, and you don't need a cable guy to install it, although aligning yourself with a guru is an excellent way to get high definition and frequent upgrades! With practice you will surely find that the picture never looked better and the standard of programming has improved tremendously!

Weather Patterns

THE COTTAGE WE RENTED DURING the summer had a spectacular view of Georgian Bay. Miles of beachfront gave the impression of it being an ocean rather than a lake. The western exposure made for nightly sunsets more compelling than any TV show. There was a television beneath the great picture window overlooking this view, but we rarely turned it on because the window made for a constantly changing scenario.

Every day the weather patterns rearranged themselves. A cacophony of waves and wind would give way to millpond surfaces and utter silence. Spectacular rain storms appeared on the horizon and leaked through the roof of our cabin. Lightning would slash the night sky, breaking up damp walls of humid air; whispering, cool breezes gave us room to breathe.

More than this, every morning as the dog and I went for our walk, I noticed that the beach was brand new. A creek that fed into the bay was re-routed by the overnight storm. Yesterday's perfect skimboarding[21] stream was today's rushing river, only to disappear to a trickle after a week of intense heat.

The dunes that sloped yesterday were level today, dressed by the wind with a new coating of pearly fine sand. A flock of geese had overnighted on a stretch of beach and used it as a public washroom. A loon came and went, giving life lessons to her chicks on land and water. It was new every moment—stormy, calm, oppressive, and invigorating, aggressive and passive, blissful and worrisome. Nature lived totally from moment to moment; it didn't hold back or second guess itself. It did what it felt compelled to do, completed with it and moved on to its next creative expression, never to repeat itself in exactly the same way.

After observing this for a while, I noticed that my moods often mimicked the weather patterns. Was I affected by the weather? Or were the same forces that affected the local climate also creating a micro-climate within the entity known as me?

When it was sunny and clear, I felt sunny and clear. When it was humid and oppressive, I was often lethargic or wilted like the flowers in the nearby planters. When it was stormy outside, I found myself restless or bothered by the noise of the wind rattling both the windows and my nerves, and like the wind howling through the trees and beating endlessly crashing waves onto the shore my mind would sometimes whine and hurl endlessly crashing thoughts against the roof of my brain.

A curious thing occurred as I explored this observation. Witness consciousness set in. Instead of being enslaved by my reactions, I became a detached witness of them—an inquisitive scientist in the laboratory of my life. I started to observe my *own* emotional weather patterns, describing them thus: "Oh look, a storm front is passing

---

21 | A board sport not unlike skateboarding but on shallow moving water near the shore's edge.

through" or "Cloudy with sunny periods" or "Looks like we're in for a long stretch of fine weather."

This had a wonderful effect on me. I stopped taking my *self* so seriously. Whatever was going on with me, just like the weather outside my window, was merely passing through, experiencing itself fully, and making way for the next weather pattern, which would then pass through, etc. Nature was experiencing the fullness of its emotional range within me as it was outside me, and just as I was in the front-row seat of the summertime adventures on the shoreline, so was I in a prime seat for the emotional and mental expressions of this life called Helen. Rather than trying to stop the storm, I simply watched it roll on through from the still point within. And then I watched the calm that followed as the storm was included and completed with.

In yoga we are told that all of *prakriti* or nature is affected by the three *gunas* or forces of nature.[22] These three forces are *satvic*, which is stillness and serenity, *rajasic*, which refers to a busy, restless nature, and *tamasic*, which is lethargic, dull, decaying, and dark in nature.

As we are part of nature, like a plant with mobile roots, these qualities also impact us, and even more so when we identify with the changing patterns. But beyond all of these changing forces remains the never-changing one, the *Purusha*. Through increasing awareness and nonjudgmental witnessing, our consciousness gradually transcends the grip of the gunas. We experience who we are in essence beyond these changing qualities, which is perfect peace and well-being, a blissful *isness*, an eternity of now.

The weather can be a great teacher when we listen to its stories!

---

[22] Sri Swami Satchidananda, *The Yoga Sutras of Patanjali, Translation and Commentary*, 1:17,18. Buckingham, VA. Integral Yoga Publications, 1990.

Flags and Original Innocence

The Georgian Bay shoreline was dotted with Canadian flags flying high from cottage flagpoles. A cottage near our rental property displayed several different flags. One was the tri-color of a European country, one was the flag of Ontario, and the other I did not recognize. Their fluttering caught my eye one breezy day, and I considered what the owners were trying to express through these colorful pieces of cloth.

They were like an acknowledgment of club membership, weren't they? They said, "I have connections to these organizations, and I am proud that I belong." There's nothing wrong with that—that is, until someone else belongs to a different club and takes offense when feeling excluded from yours. Now you have a problem. Arguments can lead to skirmishes and insults. Sides gather supporters, and quick as you can say "Twitter," you've got a full-blown war on your hands. (This goes all the way from empire colonization to religion to soccer and kids' hockey games.)

Now imagine you are way above this pretty blue planet looking down at people killing each other because of their club affiliations.

You cannot see any boundaries except those made by the oceans. Everybody fighting has a head, two arms, and two legs, so they look pretty much the same to an outsider, except maybe for the different-colored skins they are wearing. Everyone lives on the same ball floating in space, which seems to be getting grungier and bloodier by the day. Why don't they work together and clean it up, you might ask?

And why do they insist on dividing this one round ball into different sections if it only makes them rip it to shreds? Where are they planning to go after they've messed it all up? Have they thought about that? And what happens to all the guys who end up on the losing side of the skirmish? Do they get voted off the planet like an episode of the TV show *Survivor*—like there's somewhere else they can actually go? (And if there were, wouldn't they just bring their problems with them and mess that up too?) And have they thought about what will happen down the road when the sore losers tell their kids and grandchildren about the raw deal they got at the hands of the bully who didn't like their piece of cloth and who didn't want to share and play fair, and the kids feel they have to stick up for their dads and grandpas? Round and round the planet goes, where she'll stop nobody knows!

And what happens to the winners? They hold on tightly and fearfully to what they've won until the next round. They spend tremendous resources of energy and manpower to repair the damage and maintain their victory stance/dance. This selfish use of resources causes more suffering for everyone, including the winners, you observe, and is only of use until the perceived enemy comes up with a newer and more powerful way to destroy life in all its forms.

From way up high, you also notice that these little critters tend to get bent out of shape and broken from the fighting and from the natural cycle of life and death. Win or lose, their bodies are put in boxes and stuck into the same ground they were fighting over … What's up with that? Win or lose, they still die! It's not like they

FLAGS AND ORIGINAL INNOCENCE

can take it with them. The land they fight over eventually opens up and swallows them! They fight for something that eats them up *prematurely* by the very fact of their fighting for it. Am I missing something here?

Wouldn't it make sense to dispense with flags that divide rather than unite? Wouldn't it make sense to create a different type of flag or three? How about one with an image of the beautiful blue planet, the most obvious club that we all, by virtue of birth, belong to? How about another one that depicts all the planets in the cosmos, in case any aliens out there think we're being exclusive about being members of the Blue Planet Club? And finally, how about one that has a great big circle symbolizing oneness and infinity, showing the divine one life essence, the original innocence that unites every living person, place, and thing? It's all that remains when all the divisions are gone.

I wonder if my cottage neighbor would like that!

Talking Trees

On an early fall afternoon, with the sun bright and the breeze cool, my companion and I went for a hike through Eldred King Woodlands. The trees sighed and swayed, the sun flickered amidst the branches, and occasionally golden leaves floated to the soft forest floor.

We stood in a cluster of trees, listening simultaneously to the silence and the rustling, as the breeze picked up and died down. Looking up, we saw lots of movement and light. Down below, in the shade, the ferns were still, emanating calm. It seemed as though the trees whispered to each other. We felt gifted with a heavenly moment of awareness.

We moved on. I noticed the different textures of the forest. An old maple with beautiful textured bark stood beside a young, smoother version of itself. Beside it nestled a pine tree.

Identifying with the postmenopausal maple, I jokingly said to my partner, "Do you suppose the old tree resents the young one for her smooth skin?"

IN-SOURCED

To entertain my buddy and myself, I said, "Imagine the conversation if the trees had worth adequacy issues.

"Look at that young upstart, squeezing her skinny body in beside me, where there's barely any room. Who does she think she is? And just look at the way she swishes in the breeze. If she doesn't put down some roots and take life seriously, she'll surely get knocked over in the first strong gust of wind. Humph!"

I imagined another old maple nearby joining in, "And as for those pines—they are so stuck up and prickly. You can't move an inch without them jabbing you!"

"And they are *so* uptight!" responds the first. "Neither summer heat nor winter chill will make them take their clothes off! They wear the same green coat year in and year out, buttoned right up to the throat! Honestly, someone should say something! Haven't they ever heard of color? Or a good rain shower in the buff? That distinctive body odor is amazingly strong!"

They nod their branches in agreement.

Meanwhile the pine family has views of its own. "Oh my word, the first sign of fall and those slutty maples are at it again. They'll strip at the drop of a hat, tossing leaves like feather boas! Disgusting, not to mention gaudy! What is wrong with green? They can't commit to anything. Change, change, change! They just get settled being one thing when they reinvent themselves. First it's light green, they it's dark green, then red, yellow, orange, and gold. And finally, the embarrassment of it all, having to watch them stand there naked all winter long, like it's the most natural thing in the world. It's a wonder they don't freeze to death!"

Just then, the wind whisked through the poplars, setting off a sound and light show as their leaves shimmered and tapped out a staccato beat. "Show offs," I imagined the pines and maples saying in unison, surprising themselves and each other. Could they actually agree on something?

"It's good that those poplars have a short life span, considering the noisy show they put on with every passing breeze! They must think poplar means popular!"

My companion and I stood still, captivated by this very sound and light show, the vibrant leaves popping against the blue sky and silver bark.

"Do you really suppose the trees feel like that?" my partner asked, chuckling at my soap opera.

"No, absolutely not," I replied.

"How can you be so sure?" he asked.

"Close your eyes and notice how it feels here among the trees," I said.

"It's very peaceful," was his reply.

"Exactly, the harmony is palpable. If the trees were so negative and combative, it would feel different in here. We wouldn't want to stay or even come here. Perhaps they know something we don't about cohabitation. After all, they've been around a lot longer than we have."

The transference of a not-unusual human conversation onto a cast of trees outlined the absurdity of the knots in which we tie ourselves in our lives, getting upset about things that just don't matter from the perspective of the timeless universe.

Every tree is unique. They manage to live together harmoniously and even merge together as one with other trees sometimes, roots and trunks entwining. They know their place, and they live in a state of allowing. They stand around us like mighty, silent guardian angels, serving and supporting us at every step.

They shade us from the sun and protect us from the gales. They take in our waste matter and give us oxygen. They give us our food, our furniture, our paper, our homes, and our heat, even our Christmas trees … or rather they allow us to take all that without complaint or asking anything in return. They see us come, and they see us go. They even wrap around us as we are laid in our graves or help to turn us to ash if we choose to be cremated. They maintain their equilibrium by being fully themselves and by accepting that we humans are as we are.

Could we be that generous of spirit? Could we let go of our worth adequacy issues and delight in the uniqueness that we are? Could we create a magical forest of humans that vibrates with deep stillness and peace, allows everything to be as it is, and asks nothing in return?

Ask and You Shall Receive...
Just Be Wakeful How You Ask!

A**ll my childhood in Ireland** we had a nanny/housekeeper. She was wonderful and loving, and I spent a great deal of time with her. Every day after school I would sit beside her on a stool doing my homework while she ironed household linens for our large family on the kitchen table. Beside her was a brass ashtray where a lit cigarette continuously perched, sending white plumes into the air that changed shape only when interrupted by her occasional puffs. It was a comforting part of our daily ritual as she asked all about my day at school and examined me in my spelling, times tables, botany, and such. She'd pick me up for a big, bosomy hug whenever I was upset and press my face against her soft, wrinkly skin before giving me a lip-smacking kiss and putting me back down again. I loved her very much, and still do. She's in her nineties now!

Her skin was so soft and velvety and her lap so capacious, like a cozy armchair, that I felt safe from all the troubles of the world in her arms. Her hands were worn from housework, and her fingernails were yellowed from tobacco, unlike my mother's, who did not smoke. Her lips, too, were unlike my mother's. They were pleated with little vertical lines that deepened with each drag on the cigarette.

Very young, I decided that though I loved everything about her, I did not want discolored nails and wrinkled lips for myself when I grew up. I deduced that smoking must be the reason she looked like that, so I determined never to smoke! Back then nobody even knew it was bad for you.

I went through life with a semiconscious silent affirmation of, "No discolored nails for me. No wrinkled lips for me. I want nice nails and nice lips."

But here in the present day, I find myself buffing and polishing my nails to remove a perpetual discoloration that appears as the nails grow. There isn't a supplement or treatment I'm aware of that I haven't tried to rid myself of these ridged, yellowish nails. And no one has been able to tell me definitively why my nails look this way.

When I went for a facial recently, the aesthetician asked if I was a smoker. She said I have the mouth of a smoker; those little vertical lines along my top lip, you see, are a tell-tale sign. She was surprised when I said I'd never smoked!

I have been told that the universe does not understand negatives. I've also been told, "What you want leaves you wanting"[23] and the very declaration of wanting means that you are affirming that you do not have it … again and again and again. The third lesson I've learned in this vein is, "What you focus on you make more of."

Following that credo, it would seem that what the universe has been hearing from me for forty-plus years is, "Discolored nails for me, wrinkly lips for me" in conjunction with, "I affirm that I do not have nice nails and nice lips."

Now this might all seem terribly superficial if taken at face value, pardon the pun, but I was reading a book by Stacy Morrison, the

---

23 | Master Charles Cannon, Synchronicity Foundation for Modern Spirituality.

editor-in-chief of *Redbook* magazine, called *Falling Apart in One Piece*[24] when the light bulb went on concerning this lesson again. Back in 2004 she was interviewing then-President George W. Bush for the magazine. She asked him what he thought was the most-misunderstood perception the public had of him. After thinking for a few moments, he answered, "That I *long* for peace." In that moment I realized why peace has been so elusive for the last decade.

With each affirmation of longing for peace, we push it further and further from us. It affirms that we do not have it, right here, right now, in this very moment. Since this very moment is the *only* moment we ever exist, the only moment in which we have power to co-create with the universe, it becomes a tape loop recreating the same experience again and again and again and again ... Do you see where I'm going with this?

Instead of thanking the universe for the lovely little fingernails and cute little mouth that the childhood me humbly and absentmindedly exhibited, I started worrying myself into an affirmation of just the opposite from a young age. Whittling away at what I already had by making more of what I focused on leaves me where I am today. And for the record, let me state that my older sisters do not suffer from the same issues as I do. It was never their focus.

This consideration brings me to the conscious overhaul of all programmed data that is undermining my enjoyment of life. What else can I—can we as a population—change to affirm fulfillment and gratitude in the now and thus clear away years of negatively powerful wanting and longing debris?

Let me count the ways with my beautiful fingers and toes. I invite you to do likewise as I leave you with a kiss from my smooth and youthful lips!

---

24 | Morrison, Stacy. *Falling Apart in One Piece*. New York: Simon and Schuster, 2010.

IN-SOURCED

> As you think, so you become.
>
> —Sw. Satchidananda

PS: I have to add this little addendum. Wakefulness in communication is key! Just recently I was helping out in a raw food kitchen. I jokingly and not very consciously said to a colleague, "It's nice to work in a kitchen without a stove. I can't burn anything here!" *Wrong, wrong,* was I ever wrong! The universe heard (not hearing negatives), "Burn anything here."

I was asked to chop banana peppers and could only find one latex glove to protect my hands. After chopping six or eight peppers, I washed my hands. My uncovered left hand started to burn like I had stuck it in a fire and couldn't pull it out. On the bus home, I breathed and witnessed and did my best in that moment to include and allow, while noticing that my hand still burned as the night wore on. Thankfully the good citizens of Google Land provided me with a cure of applying yogurt to neutralize the spice in my skin. I slept with my hand encased in a yogurt-filled latex glove—blessed relief and a hard lesson learned. *Always* speak positively about what you choose to create. Words are powerful. Make them work for you in a beautiful way!

And when you forget, go into that space of witness consciousness that lies at the balance point between positive and negative thoughts and emotions, and see how you can detach, include, and rise above the situation. That way, every experience is appropriate and useful. Yes!

I affirm that life is an intriguing learning opportunity that increases our wisdom as long as we live with open and wakeful hearts and minds. I am willing to receive its multitude of blessings.

Are you?

What Works, What Doesn't and Do We Really Know Which Is Which?

I READ AN ARTICLE IN THE *Toronto Star* about a Toronto artist named John Newman[25] who had drawn, painted, and taught art most of his life until, at the age of seventy-eight, he had a stroke. The stroke left him paralyzed in his legs and his right hand. He was a right-handed artist. Art was his life and his creative expression of himself. He felt devastated. How would he continue to express himself?

He started to wonder about the use of his still-functioning left hand. He had none of the skill, practice, or training that faded with the stroke to the left side of his brain, but he started to draw in the air. Light strokes and imagination created images in the air as he honed his fine motor skills. Before he left rehab, he attended an art therapy session and amazed himself and everyone else with a beautiful work of art created with his left hand. His right brain has picked up where

---

25 | Debra Black, "The art of rewiring a brain", *Toronto Star*, September 27, 2011 http://www.thestar.com/entertainment/article/1060399--the-art-of-rewiring-a-brain accessed October 30, 2012

his left brain left off, but now his art has a different flavor to it. It is less solid and more subtly ephemeral, abstract, and unique. The old artist is made new, a successful artist with a beginner's mind. What seemed like a tragedy was a transformation.

I read another recent story in the same newspaper about a thirty-one-year-old up-and-coming singer and actor in Australia named Tim McCallum[26] who became quadriplegic after a diving mishap. Rather than give up his singing, which would be expected in light of his injury and lack of abdominal strength, he has navigated a way around his disability to ability. He has found the means to project his voice and entertain professionally with his powerful talent. His incredible success in vocal projection has spurred medical research in this area that will benefit so many others in a similar situation.

A few years ago I was on a meditation retreat in the mountains of Virginia. On the first evening, as I stood up out of my chair to respect the guru, Master Charles Cannon, as he entered the room, I felt a searing pain like a lightning bolt in my left calf muscle. I couldn't put my heel on the floor or place weight on my foot. This seemed most unfortunate as daily hikes through the mountains and even from building to building were an integral part of the retreat. Loving the hikes, and needing to be mobile, I wondered what I would do. How could I even meditate when I was in such pain? I took this contemplation into my seated meditation and waited for an inspiring download. Here's what I got: "You have so many body parts that work. You have one part that doesn't right now. What will you choose to focus on?"

Fair enough. I engaged in a private conversation with my calf muscle. I informed it that I was sorry it wasn't feeling well. I regretted that it was deciding to sit out the retreat, but the rest of me (and my body parts) were not about to miss out on this wonderful experience.

---

26 | Barbara Turnbull, "Tenor Tim McCallum is paralyzed – but still performing", *Toronto Star*, September 30, 2011 http://www.thestar.com/living/article/1062052--tenor-tim-mccallum-is-paralyzed-but-still-performing, accessed October 30, 2012

We would be hiking, even if it meant going on our hands and knees. We would carry it along with us, and if it felt like joining in, it was most welcome. But henceforth, we would not be focusing on its experience of pain. We would focus on the blissful surroundings and the peaceful vibrations.

At the end of the meditation I hobbled to my room on tiptoe. I took some Arnica Montana, visualized wellness, and went to bed. The next morning I limped up the mountain as inconspicuously as possible (in order to minimize concern in others that might start a conversation focused on the "dis-ease"). With each step, attention to a positive dominant focus increased with my deliberate affirmation of gratitude for what body parts were functioning well. This conscious shift of withdrawal of attention from negative dominance brought me to a midpoint of balance where all was deeply peaceful and no pain existed. I became a witnessing consciousness enjoying the play going on within and around me, something I might not have experienced had I been in perfect health. This is a tool I have used repeatedly since then when faced with ailments and injuries. Acknowledgment, inclusion, treatment if necessary, and witnessing have expanded my conscious experience of what we might call suffering. Abilities may come and go, but suffering is perhaps optional.

Did my calf muscle work or let me down? Did the strokes and paralysis work, even as the bodies failed to do what they had always done? Define work. Define transformation.

Where in your life are you dealing with obstacles that seem to be working against your desires and abilities? What are they trying to teach you? Is it possible they have come to slow you down to the speed of presence and/or spur you on to be more than you have ever been? Is it possible they are friends in disguise as adversaries?

What works, what doesn't, and are you sure you can tell the difference?

Resist nothing. Include and transcend. My spiritual mentor, Master Charles taught me that. The self transforms and flies higher than the greatest challenge, perhaps even upon the wings of it, if we allow it.

Is there some area of your life that may be creating tension and resistance? Is it possible for you to see this as a gift of transformation, nudging you to open up, welcome it in, and see what it is bringing to bless your life forever?

Isabel and the Light

Isabel comes to clean our home every two weeks. She's been coming since my grown children were little ones, when I used to work office hours. Her continued presence buys me peace of mind to meditate, teach, study, write, or go on a spiritual retreat without worrying that the house will fall apart. She is a wonderful soul, deeply spiritual, and due to her pure heart, her honest work ethic, her sharp eye, and her thoroughness, she is an in-demand, self-employed house cleaner.

She has loved my children from the very start and continues to ask after them now that they no longer live at home. She also continues to pray for them and lights candles for them at church. Not only is that a bonus you might not expect to find under the heading of "cleaning service"(though cleaning service it most certainly is, in the spiritual sense!), but she also notices things that need doing that I am blissfully oblivious to and brings my awareness to them.

"Ms. Helen," she'll say, (she prefers calling me that, despite my protestations to call me 'Helen') "the silverware needs polishing for Thanksgiving. Today I'm going to do that." Or for the last two

IN-SOURCED

visits she has said, "Ms. Helen, we need to clean the light in your bedroom."

"Oh, okay, Isabel," I'll say, and then I'll get busy with something else and forget.

Today we got the step ladder out of the garage and carried it upstairs to our bedroom. The ceiling is high. Isabel is less than five feet tall. The light in question is a crystal chandelier. To clean it is a two-person job. One person stands on top of the ladder (that would be me, who has a few inches on Isabel!) and takes off the crystals, row by row. The other person (Isabel) is at the bottom, waiting to receive them. She takes them away to wash and dry them and then returns them and awaits the next row, which I take down while she washes the previous row.

It's a beautiful light fixture (a real find at Home Depot!). It holds seventy-three crystals of varying lengths. I counted. It hangs in line with east-facing French doors. When the sun rises, it shines through the crystals and makes magical miniature rainbows on the bedroom wall. These were often the first things I would see upon opening my eyes in the morning. But in recent months we started closing the curtains—to keep the sun's heat out by day in the summer and to keep the chills out in winter. We sleep better in the darkness, but we awaken to dim light instead of rainbows at dawn.

Consequently, I was quite surprised by how dusty the light fixture was once I was nose to nose with it and proceeded to dismantle the first row of six. But I was not nearly as shocked as when Isabel brought them back all shiny and new and I hung them back up above the lower unwashed rows. What a difference! They were the same size and shape as some of the others, the same size and shape that they had been moments before, but they were completely different. Even in the dull wintry light, they shone!

"Oh my goodness, Isabel," I called out as she gently washed the next row of glass in the towel-lined bathroom sink. "These are amazing. They look so happy; I think they're smiling at me! It feels like they're singing for joy just to be able to shine again." I could feel their happiness at being able to do what came naturally to them to do, to fulfill their purpose, their *swadharma*, as we'd say in yoga.

They dazzled and winked as I twirled the chandelier to re-attach each one. I felt so happy and uplifted to be doing this job at this moment. I thanked them for shining. I thanked my eyes for seeing them shine. I thanked Isabel for making it happen.

Then the voice of wisdom within stopped me in my tracks. "This is you," it said. That's all it said, but along with those three words came a multiplicity of downloads into my conscious awareness.

"This is you. All is source. You are source. This light is source. Therefore, what you do to another you do to yourself. When you clean another, you clean yourself. As you clean this light, you, yourself become radiant." Oh!

"This is you, as in, this is mankind. We are all crystals reflecting divine light. This is our essence and our nature. But the dust of life settles upon us and dulls our glow. Over time we identify with the thick coating of dust, the enculturation, the education, the socialization, the externalization of our focus upon worldly matters, etc., and we forget we are crystal clear light. Then we settle for dullness. Our light and our life become dull, and since we no longer reflect much light, everything we perceive appears equally dull." Oh!

No wonder cleaning the glass drops made me feel so happy and yes, light. I kept this information to myself as we continued with our work. The finished product was a de-light to behold, even before we switched it on. Yes!

As I drove Isabel home after work, I felt buoyant and ecstatic. I thanked her once more for her persistence in pushing me to complete this task with her and for the joy she gave me with its beautiful result (not even mentioning what it had taught me).

"Oh, Ms. Helen," she said. "No need to thank me. I feel *so* happy we did this. You know," she said, "it's weird, but I feel *so* clean!"

Yes, Isabel, I know exactly how you feel.

In Memoriam

Today is November 26, 2011. It feels like a birthday of sorts for me—my third birthday, to be precise. It's the day when death came so close I could smell its fiery breath[27]. It came so close it took away four of those who were gathered nearest to me. It struggled desperately with those just a few feet away from me, but they wriggled, injured, from its grasp. It laid a finger on me but barely made a dent.

November 26 is the day life wrapped itself around me with even greater protective love than before and told death, clearly and firmly, "No, she's mine, and you can't have her just yet. Leave her in her body for now. Leave her alone."

This was the second time in 2008 that life had done this for me. At the beginning of the year, in February, during a very early-morning walk, death shoved me from behind and sent me sailing through the air. I landed with a thud in an icy ravine, snapping my pelvis like a twig. I distinctly heard and felt the crack. As I lay there on a slope

---

27 | For more information go to www.ahyogahh.com/news/media or Master Charles Cannon. *Forgiving The Unforgivable*, New York, Select Books Inc. 2011.

of ice and snow below road level, my temperature dropping in the freezing temperature and unable to move or attract help (and dressed all in white, which made me blend in with the surrounding scene), life, at my request, sent my (white!) dog off up to the road to find someone to take care of me. A complete stranger was my guardian angel that day, along with my lifesaver west highland terrier, Eugene, who brought the kind man down to me. In retrospect I feel this first attempt might have been a dress rehearsal to prepare me for what happened in India, giving me the rehabilitation period I needed to contemplate and meditate on life, death, and my relationship with both and with the divine. It gave me time to separate the important from the unimportant.

Here in Markham, when crisis struck and I found myself alone (except for my devoted dog), life stepped in and handled everything.

In India, when crisis struck and I found myself alone, all my friends either dead, severely injured, or under siege in their hotel rooms, life stepped in and took care of me through the wonderful efforts of bright souls.

For some reason, life seems to love me, to want to cherish me and meet all my needs. It seems to want me to stick around and not to worry about anything. It says, "I've got your back. I've got it covered. Just be. Just be. Be love. Be happy. Be joy. Be with me. Let's play together."

I love life and am grateful to it for all its precious gifts. And one of those precious gifts is you!

Life seems to want me to tell you that it has your back too, that it wants the same for you ... if you will just allow it to take its course and watch and trust what happens moment by moment. And when the time is right for death to claim the body, it will come and get us, and what a wondrous experience that will be too!

Victory to life, which is eternal! Victory to death, which is just a change in the vehicle we ride! Victory to love, which is the power behind it all!

Jai (victory) to my dear friends Alan and Naomi Scherr for teaching us so much with their sudden and unexpected graduation from the body in Mumbai. Jai!

In your unique experience of life, can you be chill (without having to fall down a frozen ravine or get shot at in a hotel in India!) and allow life to live you and to love you?

Awareness That Space Is God

Space includes all and everything
And never suppresses
Space allows us to make love
Or war
While holding us in its gentle embrace

Space allows the notes to play
The words to speak
The dancer to dance

Space allows the river to run
And the sun, held lovingly in its arms,
To shine

Space blows gentle kisses of breeze
Upon my face
And sends a river of blood flowing
Through my veins

IN-SOURCED

Space is within me and all around me
It is the breath of air
And also the lung

My cells expand in its care
I am more space than cell
I *am* space
I *am* God
My awareness makes me one.

In-Sourcing and the Upward Facing Dog

> Dog is God spelled backwards.
>
> —Sw. Satchidananda

Sometimes very special souls wander into our lives, or we into theirs, in the middle of an ordinary day. Sometimes they wander in on four legs and change our lives forever. A fluffy, white west highland terrier puppy named Eugene with enormously disproportionate ears was one of those.

From the moment he locked eyes with my kids and me through the glass in the pet store window (yes, the pet store—it was thirteen years ago and we didn't know any better, thank God), it was a bridge too far, or at the very least a definite maybe. Then when I held him in my arms it felt like our two hearts clicked together as one puzzle piece. After a moment of blissful stillness, a unified sigh escaped us both, and there was no turning back. Life is made new in the everyday moments as eternity devises a new play and a new lesson plan.

Eugene came with a whole "universe-ity" degree list of courses, just a few of which I'll touch on here. Through his tuition we earned credits in unconditional love, patience, contentment, trust, courage, optimism, adventure, compassion, presence and simplicity, the pure joy of living, togetherness, and more. His gifts are long-lasting and priceless.

We thought 2008 was an *annus horribilis* for our family (otherwise known as the Year of the Quantum Leap in Consciousness). Now with the benefit of hindsight, I tend to view it more as an *annus mirabilis*. As I mentioned in the "In Memoriam" contemplation, I managed to fall and break my pelvis while out walking Eugene early one morning, 7:30 a.m. on February 29, to be exact. The irony of that date was not lost on me—to take a flying leap down an icy ravine on Leap Day proved that Providence had not lost its sense of humor!

Not only did Eugene take it upon himself to go find help that morning, but he also brought his co-life saver back down the ravine to where I lay, unable to move. He then proceeded to back up onto me—half-sitting on me—and quietly growled at the kind gentleman who came to my aid when he reached out to touch me, as if to say, "I've got the touching part covered. Please keep your hands off her and call 911. Thank you very much."

Dramatic though the morning was, there was more to come. I collapsed soon after returning home. I had climbed to the top of the stairs, with the aid of my husband and son, on my way to rest in bed, when I saw a subtle vision of pink- and golden-colored orbs, floating in the air like giant champagne bubbles, along with experiencing a flash of nausea and lightheadedness. I said to my husband, "I'm either going to be sick or I'm going to …"

The next thing I knew I was in a state of exquisite bliss, like when I am in deepest meditation but unlike meditation in that I was surrounded by brilliant whiteness. All that existed was my awareness and this lovely white light. I was completely and utterly at peace and ecstatic. I had the feeling I must be sitting in the lotus position on my meditation bench, except that I felt like I was floating above it rather than upon it. I was content to remain like this forever. Home at last!

After some time (my husband tells me it was a few minutes), I became aware of someone trying to kiss me. *Kiss me? Who would disturb this wonderful meditation by trying to kiss me?* I was not impressed, as I felt myself being pulled out of my ecstatic state, and I most definitely did not want to leave it.

The next thing I knew I was lying on my bed. *How did I get here? Wasn't I just at the top of the stairs? How come I am not on my meditation bench?* The kissing turned out to be my husband performing CPR on me after he and my son had carried me to bed. At the foot of the bed, my son stood talking on the telephone to the 911 operator. What in the world was going on?

After my brief visit to the realm of near-death experiences, I was back in the land of the living, for better or for worse. It appeared I was not done yet.

It took three months to recover from that injury, and Eugie rarely left my side, spending every moment he was allowed, on the bed beside me until I was able to get up and move around again.

Whenever I sat to meditate, he would sit right beside me, his little bum pressed against my leg as though plugging in for a connection to the higher wattage power. I wondered if he was sending me healing or looking for some meditative bliss of his own. I could feel his devotion, as if my well-being were his sole mission in life at that time.

As I also mentioned earlier, November of 2008 was when the Mumbai terrorist attacks happened. Some of my dear friends were killed, but I survived (once again, profoundly calm in the eye of the storm as source guided me from within)—apparently *still* not done yet! Also, in the fall of that year, my husband's mother, who lived in Ireland, was diagnosed with terminal brain cancer. Just after I returned from Mumbai, my family and I departed for Ireland to visit with her before Christmas. We had to return again in February 2009 for her funeral, where I injured myself again—almost a year to the day after my first treacherous fall.

It's safe to say my family and I did a lot of emotional processing in 2009 and decided to rent a cottage up north during the summer holidays for some much-needed rest and relaxation. The only problem was that the landlady did not want any pets. What to do with our baby?

I found a doggie vacation resort on the Internet not too far from where we were staying. If we put Eugie there we could visit him occasionally. It seemed nice on the web. The owner was reassuring over the phone. We signed him up for his own spa vacation.

It didn't feel so right when we got there, though. All the other dogs were very large breeds and well-acquainted with each other. They seemed to be eager to show Eugene who was boss. Although the place was fenced and the owner assured me he'd be fine once we left, I just didn't feel good about the place or the person. I was getting a very unsafe vibe. I told myself I was just re-living my kids' first days at kindergarten and ignored my intuition, judging it to be helicopter parenting!

Curiously, my husband, who is generally much more pragmatic and logical than I, didn't feel great about leaving him there either. But we wondered what else we could do at that point, and the owner assured us it wouldn't be a problem. Reluctantly, we drove away but not before I told the lady I would call later to check how he was settling in—assuming my cell phone had reception in that area. I also gave her my husband's usually more reliable cell number.

I couldn't get Eugie out of my mind all the rest of the day (Saturday) but resisted the urge to call. She hadn't called us, so he must be okay, right?

By Sunday afternoon, I couldn't stand it any longer. I called.

She answered, "Oh, I've been trying to reach your husband's phone, but I'm not getting through."

"Why? Is everything okay?" I asked, trying to quell the rising tide of fear with calm breathing.

She replied, "Well, he got out yesterday afternoon about two hours after you left. We can't find him anywhere!"

I said, in denial, "I thought you said your place was secure! How did that happen?"

She said, "He pushed a hole through the chicken wire fence and dug and squeezed his way through. My husband saw a white dog loose in the neighborhood and told me he'd found him, but when I double checked a few hours later, it was the wrong dog—not yours."

Feeling my mind explode with incomprehension, I said, "Your husband picked up someone else's dog?"

She said, "I'm afraid so. He knew your dog was white, so he assumed it must be him."

I replied, "We'll be right over."

Thus began the hellish start to our recuperative family vacation. We were up in northern Ontario in an unfamiliar place. We did not know our way around this relative wilderness where all manner of wild animals were the resident experts, but more to the point, neither did Eugene, who was now wandering *lost* and totally exposed to the elements!

My Mumbai experience immediately kicked in as the family started to fear the worst.

"Why is this happening to us again?" asked my son, referring to the experience they went through the November before, not knowing for a brief period whether I was dead or alive. I knew there must be a lesson in this. The universe knows what it's doing. Was there something that needed to be completed after Mumbai?

"Let's not assume what we do not know for sure," I said. "We are here. It is now. Eugene is not at his kennel. That's all we know. We have to consciously choose positivity right now. If we're going to assume, let's assume the best—and give it to God for the highest

IN-SOURCED

good. Let's not feed the fear with our attention. Indifference to the wicked,"[28] I added, quoting one of my often-repeated lines from the four locks and keys of the Yoga Sutras of Patanjali.

All agreed, though conscious of the hungry knot of fear in our stomachs that was aching to be fed. We spent hours scouring the surrounding area, canvassing residents and gas stations, and leaving our numbers in case anyone spotted him. Some said they'd seen a white dog walking along Highway 12—the main highway!

After dark, we returned to our cottage. I closed my eyes and could feel Eugie in my arms. I sensed that he was alive and sent him my love. I knew he was wearing his Town of Markham license tag. He was also wearing his rabies tag with a contact number for his vet on it. Since my phone worked and incredibly my husband's lacked reception, I would call first thing on Monday morning and alert both parties.

For now, all I could do was meditate and trust. I had brought sacred ash (*vibuthi*) with me from Sathya Sai Baba's ashram that had been gifted to me after the attack in India, along with a picture of Sai Baba with the caption: "I never ask that you earn me. I only want that you need me." Well, I needed Baba now …

I put some of the fragrant ash in my mouth and on my head to help me center and focus and spent the night sitting up in meditation, praying to Sai Baba and all the sages and saints to save my little dog, as they had saved me twice before.

"I need your help and your perspective, Baba. In your enlightening state, you have a better vantage point of the whole scenario. I am too close emotionally and on the ground. Please tell me what's going on."

Inwardly I asked my friend Alan, who had been killed in India, if Eugene was with him. "He's not here," he replied, to my relief.

---

28 | Sri Swami Satchidananda *The Yoga Sutras of Patanjali*. Buckingham, Virginia: Integral Yoga® Publications 1987 Second Edition 1990, Page 54, 1:33: "By cultivating attitudes of friendliness toward the happy, compassion for the unhappy, delight in the virtuous, and disregard toward the wicked, the mind-stuff retains its undisturbed calmness".

IN-SOURCING AND THE UPWARD FACING DOG

In the quietness of the night and the stillness of meditation, Sai Baba appeared in my inner awareness.

"He's in good hands," he said. "He's safe, just very excited."

First thing in the morning I called the vet's office and asked them to notify me if anyone called them to report a found dog. I did the same with the Town License Office. I called another friend of mine who is gifted to commune with souls, living and passed on. He assured me Eugene was still alive and in the surrounding area. That confirmed Sai Baba's and Alan's messages and my own intuition. I clung to absolute faith while surrendering the whole story for the highest good.

A few hours later, we got a call from the vet's office. A lady had called them to say her daughter had spotted a dog trotting down the highway the previous afternoon as she was on her way to work. She pulled over, picked him up, and brought him to her parents. They lived in another town over. We got the address and directions and set off in high spirits, feeling sure that he must be a hungry mess after his adventure in the wild.

We got there to be greeted by a lovely couple and one immaculately clean, happy, and excited dog.

The man told us Eugene was so hyper when he first got there that he relieved himself on the floor and insisted on following the man wherever he went, even into the bathroom.

"He was so dirty," said the lady, "that I gave him a bath and trimmed his beard, which was all black from his digging."

Eugene, the yogi dog, had very clearly decided he was not safe there (as my husband and I had feared) and epitomized the power of intention, fearlessness, courage, and determination to do whatever it took to get back to his family. He headed down the highway he had come up just hours earlier and was ready to walk as long as it took and to face possible death in pursuit of realizing that intention. Dedicated, loving, positive, and trusting in the innate goodness of life and his own radiant presence, he instead got pampered and groomed in a very different kind of spa and ended up spending the rest of the vacation cuddling in bed and communing with us at the cottage (which I suspect is what he wanted all along) after the astonished landlady heard our traumatic tale.

Sai Baba had been exactly right. Eugene had been "very excited and in very good hands."

And we had received profound lessons in trusting our intuition and the power of meditation or in-sourcing. Connecting with the divine showed that universal love and consciousness are there for us no matter how impossible the situation—no Internet or telephone line required. Yes!

Three years later, the plan and the lessons have changed again. Eugene passed away peacefully at home after a long illness on summer solstice this year 2012, just shy of his thirteenth birthday. The new plan involves letting go, and the lesson is learning how to adjust to life without the touch of his warm cuddly body and the sound of his feet on the hardwood floor. Yet this lesson also brings the palpable awareness of his loving presence still with us in our home, in our dreams and forever in our hearts.

PS: I would like to thank all those who came to my rescue, and also Eugene's during that remarkable year. You know who you are. By extension, your acts of kindness saved the whole family. May countless blessings be yours.

People of the World Untie

A CARTOON DREW ITSELF IN MY head during meditation recently. I wish I could draw it for you as it appeared to me, but I'm not talented as a cartoonist, so I'll do my best to draw it with words.

Picture this:

> The sun is coming up, signifying the dawn of a new age. In front of it a guru-like figure stands with hands in the air and calls forth, "People of the world, unite!"

The next image is of planet earth. It shows what looks like a large group of people moving toward the guru. But upon closer inspection, we see that the gathering is moving very clumsily, their movements hampered by the giant crutches that are tied to their bodies. They trip, stumble, crawl, and fall repeatedly over these awkward crutches. Are these human beings or zombies? Where is their structural integrity?

IN-SOURCED

The next images focus on the crutches themselves. Words are scrawled upon each one, and the people seem to be carrying things in their hands. Obese people stagger under plates piled with food carried in one hand while strapped onto the *food* crutch by the other hand. Others stagger with bottles of wine, spirits, and beer, using the *alcohol* crutch to prop themselves up. Some crutches are made in the shape of giant hypodermic needles. These are tied to their arms with rubber strips. *Tobacco* reads one; *workaholic*, another; *sex addiction, sports addiction*, and *caffeine* still others.

Another looks like an automatic weapon. It reads *power*. Some have giant televisions tied to their crutches. Some stagger on high stilettos, dragging suitcases of fancy clothes, tripping on the *fashion* and *shopping* crutch. Others crash into things while talking and texting on cell phones and using their *techno* crutches to lug computers. Some even have several of the aforementioned crutches tied to their bodies. These are hemmed in on all sides, giving the appearance of prison bars. They can barely move.

The next picture shows people unable to move at all as they are tied to large gates that guard expensive homes, cars, and possessions, with *money* piled up in mountains in the gardens of these homes. In some instances, entire groups seem to be tied together, fenced by the *family, corporation, religion,* and *conformity* crutches.

Everyone is bumping and jostling against each other, so ungraceful are their attempts at following the guru's instruction. Very few appear able to stand on their own two feet and move freely without some sort of prop.

> What a strange and sad sight! Puzzled, the guru turns to the rising sun of source and asks, "Is *this* what you created? Where are all the empowered free spirits?"

Turning back to the crowds, the guru scratches his head and tries again: "People of the world," he cries out, "*un-tie!*"

We begin our existence as free spirits, whole and content for no reason, but due to societal, educational, religious, political, familial, and media enculturation, we forget. We buy into the accepted theory that we are somehow lacking and incomplete. This distances us from our inner true self and its voice of sanity and support. Instead we dismiss it and listen to the voice of insanity that comes from outside us, in many cases without stopping to consider that most of those who tell us we're not good enough or that we need something to be happy have a vested interest in our disempowerment (or are projecting their own feelings of inadequacy upon us). What an unbelievably successful scam!

We willingly **give away** our freedom and our power so that others can make money from us and control us, dictating what we "need" to be okay. The question is, if they *really knew* what they were talking about, and if what they said were true, shouldn't we and *they* be happy and fulfilled by now?

I don't buy water heaters from sketchy individuals who show up at my door who just want my money tied into a contract that I don't want or need ... do you? So why, I ask you, do we buy fear and disempowerment without a second thought from a multitude of powers that be who profit from our misery when we could choose self-mastery, freedom, and fulfillment that surpasses anything money could buy? We could be happy for no reason simply because we are naturally created that way.

I'm not saying that we have to live in hair shirts in the desert; not at all. I'm saying the way out is in. Meditate to find the vast completeness of your own true self, which is the missing puzzle piece that we seek elsewhere in an effort to fill the emptiness inside. Once you are at home in your own self and live according to its internal guidance, then the toys of the world can be enjoyed as passing entertainment

IN-SOURCED

and not an addiction that we have to hook up to in order to feel happy or adequate.

Attachments steal our happiness. The Bhagavad Gita[29] tells us: "The pleasure that arises when the senses contact the sense objects seems at first to be nectar, but in the end is bitter as poison."[30] The first drink, drug, smoke, piece of chocolate cake, love affair, or casino visit comes to mind. With time what you thought you owned ends up owning you. (And as an aside, how would you feel tomorrow if some catastrophe suddenly prevented all accessibility to your crutches ... pretty distressed maybe?)

It also says: "Pleasure that at first seems like poison, but in the end is nectar is pure joy arising in the clear mind of Self-realization."[31] Think of switching from junk food to fruit and veggies, your first ever work-out/yoga/meditation experience, which at first was challenging, but ultimately liberating and empowering. To *need* nothing is to enjoy everything.

Self-awareness and self-responsibility may not initially be as attractive as conforming mindlessly to the mentality of the masses, but wouldn't you rather be free, strong, and gracefully self-empowered?

We don't need crutches! We just need to look deeply into the mirror of meditation and see the one we are looking for, looking back at us.

People of the world untie, indeed. When we are all untied and untangled, we will see that we are already united! Yes!

---

29 | Commentary by Sri Swami Satchidananda. *The Living Gita, The Complete Bhagavad Gita*. Buckingham, Virginia. Integral Yoga® Publications. 1988. 3rd Printing 1997
30 | Bhagavad Gita 18:38. Page 275
31 | Ibid., 18:37. Page 274

A Blissful Christmas

M<small>Y PRAYER FOR</small> C<small>HRISTMAS IS</small> love, bliss, peace, health, wealth, and happiness in the true experience of Christ consciousness for you and for all.

Speaking of prayers, one of my teachers, Suresh Goswamy,[32] taught me that every sincere prayer is always answered. The question is what is a sincere prayer? You don't have to be on your knees with your hands pressed together, pleading and bargaining with a God out there somewhere.

A sincere prayer is like a butterfly escaping the chrysalis of the heart to soar to the heavens. It has two wings: sincere intention and strong feeling. I'll give you an example.

My husband, Dan, and I were at Sheridan nurseries recently buying our Christmas tree. Dan suggested we go inside the store first to see all the festive decorations. He knows I'm a sucker for cute and cuddly animals, real, mechanical, or stuffed. I was mesmerized (like a kid at Christmas!) by all the lovely creatures ... but a life-sized deer

---

[32] Suresh Goswamy is a teacher of raja yoga and founder of Yoga & Meditation Studios of Canada, based in Markham, Ontario. See Resources for more information.

took my breath away, especially when it lifted its head and looked at me with its big, dark eyes.

"Oh, how beautiful you are," I said spontaneously, as I reached out to stroke its faux fur. "I wish I could take you home with me."

Now, to be truthful, I have no room for a life-sized mechanical deer, nor could I afford its astronomical price ($3,000+)! But mechanical or not, I felt the love. What can I say? God (or source) hides behind every face, and I wanted to commune with it!

Shortly after returning home, I was sitting in the living room, reading a book when Dan called to me quietly from the garden. I could tell from his whispered shout of "Helen," that I'd better come quickly and quietly. Now what do you think I saw when I opened the back door?

Yes indeed, one real life-sized deer with her baby grazing by her side was looking at us right over the black metal fence of our backyard. As the two of us and Eugene looked on in amazement, she held our gaze for the longest time with her big, dark eyes, exactly like the deer in the store! We were speechless—that is, until Eugene found his voice and gave a little bark of, "Show's over folks. Time to move it along," whereupon the two of them ambled down the ravine to the water's edge and grazed some more. Even from there she turned and looked back up at us for quite some time, as if she was trying to communicate something! It was a priceless experience for Dan and me ... and who knows maybe it was for the deer too!

My sincere prayer had escaped from my heart and flown to the heavens, and the response was almost immediate. I wish the same for you this season. May your fervent wishes take flight and create magical moments in your life and in the lives of those you love.

What Is God Worth to You?

I thought I would deliver to you some soul-searching questions to declutter the mind. Take all the time you need to consider each one. Watch the inner guidance that asserts itself. Remember, everything is appropriate. Your entire life experience has brought you to this moment. The choices you make now will determine your next moments. Appreciate the power you have to shape your experience of wholeness or fragmentation, happiness or misery. You are powerful beyond measure!

Now to the wakeful stuff:

If you were to rate God/source (i.e., your relationship with divinity, the experience of your own divinity) on a scale of your top ten priorities, would it even make the list?

What does God mean to you? Does this question inspire delight or dread, guilt, disinterest, enthusiasm, or a reluctant sense of drudgery? Is God inside you, one with you or way out there in the blue yonder? Have you any idea what that divine relationship might look like?

IN-SOURCED

Is God something you discarded around puberty when you chose to pursue happiness and fulfillment through the material myth of mass consumption and sensory gratification? Have you succeeded in your pursuit of *lasting* fulfillment by going that route?

Sri Swami Satchidananda said, "Your peace is the God within you. Don't give it away for trifles."

Can you say that this is true for you? Does the experience of deep inner peace make it regularly to your top ten lists of experiences? Or are more vexing dramas taking over the coveted spots, and if so, why? Do you think these dramas will buy you happiness? Do you think they are worth throwing away your peace of mind for?

If you want to know what people's real values are, don't ask them; watch them. If you want to know what your real values are, just watch yourself. Watch what comes out of your mouth in your words, from your thoughts. (I am speaking to myself here too, as much as to you. It's an ongoing process.) What do you habitually think about and talk about? Br. Anandamoy of Self-Realization Fellowship tells us that we think 60 percent of the *same* thoughts *every day!* That makes it easy to identify the main focus of your attention! Would you say your thinking is inclusive and holistic or exclusive and divisive?

Watch what goes into your body in terms of food and liquid, smoke, pills, or other drugs and with what regularity. There's no judgment here. It's a laboratory experiment, merely taking notes and making observations about what works and what doesn't in terms of bringing you lasting happiness or unhappiness. Does the consumption of the aforementioned lead you to a state of constant balance and wholeness? Does it make you feel better or worse in the long run?

Watch how you spend your moments each day. Do you wake up every morning blissful and grateful for another day to experience life in a human form along with all the gifts that the day holds for you? Or do you resist the day, put your head down, and struggle to get through it, and if so, why? What unhappiness and illusion underlie such an attitude? What, as my mentor, Master Charles Cannon, would say, is the causative factor of this? (Is it those mostly negative stories that you focus on for 60 percent of each day, every day?) Can you be with what is, in an inclusive way, without judgment or wishing that it be other than it is but instead merely watching the play unfold as you sit contentedly and neutrally in the audience of witness consciousness, being open to possibility and intuitive direction? (I didn't say it was easy!)

I was taken aback recently to read a quotation of Swami Satchidananda's (I can't remember where) where he said he never did anything he didn't want to do in his life! Is that true for you? I contemplated this for a while as here in the West we seem to spend a great deal of time doing what we would prefer not to do. Why should it be different for Swamiji?

Then I read the writings of Dr. Edward Bach,[33] the creator of the Bach Flower Remedies, where he said that the greater the gap between the soul and the mind (ego), the greater the propensity for disease (emotional dis-ease, which, left unresolved, results in physical or mental disease).

Now I understood the guru's comment. Sw. Satchidananda was raised in a deeply spiritual family in India. All of life was prioritized upon one's relationship with the God within. All decisions were guided by the soul and not the ego. His life had integrity. There was no gap. His decisions and choices were based upon integrity—on what was for the highest good of all in each moment.

When the unenlightened ego is in charge, we live in a house divided, which is the very opposite of integrity. Simply put, the ego is selfishly not interested in what the soul has to say, as it fears its loss of power if the soul becomes dominant. It actually has a vested interest in keeping the house divided. It concocts all kinds of stories

---

33 | Bach, Dr. Edward. *The Bach Flower Remedies, Revised Edition.* New Canaan, Connecticut: Keats Publishing, Inc., 1997, Page 10.

to distract the mind from the very presence of the soul within. These entertaining stories can take lifetimes to unravel and drag us further and further from the awareness of the worth of God (which is our innate divinity and natural state of being).

We start to put all our energy into putting out fires in our lives and climbing competitive mountains. If only … then I'll be whole, then I'll be happy. But somehow another fire always erupts and … well, there's just never any time for focusing on inner peace, is there? By our actions we show that God just isn't worth very much, though our words might disagree, and we have excuses and stories aplenty to back up our words.

If we want to get really clear and honest, life and its priorities become very simple. Put peace first. Keep it there. Be prepared to make everything else secondary. Be prepared to make changes in your life to accommodate peace, and be prepared for changes to occur spontaneously around you as your thoughts, words, and actions align with this peace. Meditate, meditate, and meditate some more. Choose balance over imbalance.[34]

Then you'll gradually come to know at the very depths of your soul what God is worth to you. This will be an experience, not a conceptual belief. Be clear, be focused; be courageous. Be firm in your intention. Be regular in your practice. Watch miracles happen. Be the embodiment of peace. Be the God that you are. Don't settle for any more fakes.

---

[34] "The means gather around a pure intention" —Maharishi Mahesh Yogi, by way of Alan Scherr.

A Life In Clothes: Living the Material Myth

Spirit lowering
*

Naked and free
*

Diapers and bibs
Comfy, soft, and washable
Easy access for body spills
And messy cleanups by grown-up hands
*

Sturdy shoes for growing feet
Socks pulled up and tie on straight
Scratchy woolen sweaters
Stiff shirt collars
Cotton knickers with my name ironed on
Rubber boots and school berets
*

Denim jeans and snow white Ts

IN-SOURCED

Wild hair and no brassiere
Maxi skirts and lots of beads
Shaving and shoes optional
*

High heels and seamed hose
Push-up bras and lace panties
Tight skirts and shapely tops
Long, painted nails and groomed locks
Diamonds, pearls, and earrings that dangle
*

Travel garments and exotica
*

Sweats with spit-up
Stretch waistlines
Jeans for convenience
Sneakers and slip-ons
Earrings left in the box
Safe from tiny fingers
Nails cut short and bare
Hair tied up and out of the way
Lip balm and mascara
*

Work uniform(ity)
*

Nails grow long
The kids are gone
Time now to groom
High heels for the theater
Glasses for reading
Dress as you please
And dry clean
Elegance, fitness, and ease

*

Travel garments and exotica
*

Diapers and bibs
Comfy, soft, and washable
Easy access for body spills
And messy cleanups by grown-up hands
*

Naked and free
*

Then
Sunday best
A wooden box
A wrap of earth and grass
Or a Grecian urn
*

Spirit soaring
*

Adapt, Adjust, Accommodate

When Swami Satchidananda's guru, Swami Sivananda, was asked to speak of the essence of yoga he said the following: "Be good, do good, love all, serve all. Adapt, adjust, accommodate. Bear insult, bear injury, highest yoga."

"Now why would he say such a thing?" you might ask yourself. "Okay, I see the point in being and doing good. Fair enough, I can try to do that."

Love all. Serve all ... "Well, I'm not quite as sure about this," you say. "Some people are just too difficult to love, so I'll have to think about this for a while."

Adapt, adjust, accommodate ... "Well now, look here," you might say. "I've spent most of my life doing just that, and all I've gotten is walked on. I'm not doing that anymore. Sorry, Swamiji. Let others adapt, adjust, and accommodate to me and my needs for a change."

Bear insult, bear injury, highest yoga ... "What? Why should I let some ignoramus insult me and do nothing about it? Where's the value in that? Isn't that allowing an act of violence, verbal or physical, to be perpetrated upon me? How can that be yogic? How can it be right to allow someone to get away with hurting my feelings or my person?"

These are all valid responses ... from an egoic perspective, which is fragmented and illusory and sees all and everything as separate and different from itself.

However, as yoga comes from the Sanskrit *jug*, meaning to yoke, join, or unite, the essence of yoga comes from a perspective of unified consciousness. Think about that for a moment—a unified perspective. That means there is no other. The other is also part of the unified consciousness, another facet in the multi-faceted diamond that is source itself. The same consciousness flows through and gives life to everything. We are united, though we may not see the life force connecting us all.

Master Charles sometimes uses the analogy of the human body. From a fragmented perspective, the finger might consider itself to be completely separate and different from the head. It might gang up with the other fingers with whom it identifies and say, "Off with the head!" simply because it was insulted by what the mouth had to say about its chipped nail, for example. But the finger and the head are really part of one body, and what you do to one part influences and affects all the other parts. Get a thorn in the finger and the head is aware of the pain. In fact, chances are it won't feel content until the thorn is removed from the finger. Do you see how it works? Of course, if the hand starts violently slapping the face, then the face is justified, out of self-survival and self-respect, to move away from the hand or have it restrained to protect its safety. But it can do so lovingly and without becoming bitter and vengeful.

All of Swamiji's directives are based not on a holier-than-thou philosophy of showing the world what a good person you are. (This would be egotistical.) They are magical tips on how to create and maintain peace and love in your own life. Whatever you do, good or bad, affects you just as much as the illusory other. If we hurt someone else, on some level we feel the pain, or will in the future when we evolve and are more wakeful.

So why would you want to do anything else to yourself or have anyone else do to you other than: be good, do good, love all, serve all, adapt, adjust, and accommodate? You are only ever dealing with yourself. It's in your own interest to send as much love and compassion to yourself as possible, if this is the experience you would choose for yourself. Don't sow negativity or suffering that you will have to reap now or later!

As for bearing insult and injury—well, it is usually the ego that reacts to insults because it identifies with the shell of itself rather than the essence and seeks to project a certain image. When someone insults us and we are attached to that particular self-image, it may sting. This insult then becomes a growth experience for us to see what illusions we are holding onto and identified with. It brings them to the surface of our awareness so we can include and transcend them and free ourselves from needless baggage.

If, however, we notice someone insulting us and it doesn't sting, we see it is an indicator of the ignorance of the insulter, showing that he or she knows no better in that moment. We are given an opportunity to return an unkind act with kindness. It allows us to see that we are growing and evolving on our holistic journey, so we can silently thank our insulters for allowing us to pass an unexpected test and wish them well on their own journeys from dense dimensional awareness to a more subtle and enlightened consciousness.

Now isn't that better than an unconscious mud-slinging match? You get to walk away clean, whole and peaceful and send a ray of light back to the darkness. Darkness simply cannot exist if everyone sends light to it.

I would like to leave you with a contemplation of the "Love all, serve all" dictum. Remember that "all" includes you. Therefore we must strive to remember not to insult, injure, or disrespect *ourselves* in any way but to love and delight in the truthful light of source creation that we are. Isn't it nice to know you can always count on yourself for unconditional love and respect? Start from here and the rest will be easier. Just adapt, adjust, and accommodate.

As I mentioned in a previous contemplation, Swami Satchidananda said a perfect yogic act is one that benefits at least one person and harms no one, *including oneself*. Think about that.

When you *really* love yourself, it's just not enticing to *not* love anyone else in a compassionate way; it disturbs the balance of mind too much, which steals our natural state of easeful, peaceful, blissful being.

How does this feel to you? Are you up to the challenge of the peaceful holistic warrior?

Decisions, Decisions

How You Choose To Make Your Decisions Will Affect Their Outcome And Thus Your Life

It seems like several members of our household are in transition these days and have to make decisions about what to do and how to be next. There is nothing unusual here as it is the nature of life to keep changing and evolving. There are several ways to go about making decisions. You could choose to be selfish and dictatorial, as in: "This is how I see it, and this is how I stand to gain the most from this. Therefore this is how it is and what I'm going to do. I'm right. They're wrong. End of story, and who cares about everyone else."

You could choose to be collaborative, discussing your issue with everyone, seeing what they want you to do, and working toward pleasing as many people as you can without taking your own needs into consideration, as in: "It's all right—as long as they're happy and they like me and need me, I'll manage, so I'll do that."

IN-SOURCED

Both of these methods are of the mind and egotistical, one aggressively so and one passively so. Neither is likely to buy you much peace of mind in the long term.

Another method is simply not to make a decision at all. Put the issue out of your head. Deny there is one. Have a smoke or a drink, eat something, or go watch a movie or sports event if and when the issue pops into conscious awareness. Push it back down into suppression with the tool of your choice, until all hell breaks loose from internal stress spilling out into the external expression of chaos or ill health in your life. Ouch! This way, like the other choices mentioned above, has got to hurt. It is the unconscious process, like taking the slow boat to China and being vaguely seasick the whole time ... painful but sometimes inevitable.

Or you could take your challenge into meditation. Go into the stillness, away from external distraction and mental static and the opinions of others. Inwardly write your issue on the blackboard of consciousness, ask for inspiration, *listen deeply* to the intuition that comes in the silence, and evaluate that, see how it feels. Try your possible decision on in your imagination and see if it increases or decreases peace of mind.

I often imagine an internal energy elevator in my body and see whether it climbs up to the penthouse or down to the basement as I imagine different options. Fear-based decisions tend to crash, and love-based choices elevate to higher levels.

Don't be surprised if the decision that feels right is not the logical or rational choice. Inner guidance can see further around corners than we can, and my experience and practice of going with the intuitive choice has personally shown me that, if I jump the net will appear.

Trust is required to make this choice. But then, trust is required no matter what decision you make, so I'd rather trust a download from universal consciousness than groupthink or being rational, which is not at all the same thing as being wise.

I was pondering this idea in bed last weekend when an intuitive download just announced itself. It said, and I quote, "People who make their decisions based only on external opinions and personal gains are like popularity cliques and bullies in the school yard. They forfeit their power and integrity to an ignorant master."

Unquestioned, this kind of decision making leads to disasters throughout history, from lynch mobs to wars to segregation, colonization, isolation, and marginalization of every sort and the effects of these decisions continue today with economic, political, social, and religious upheaval.

I have heard Master Charles Cannon advocate that we move away from the herd mentality and be a "radical cow." Seek your own shade in order to keep your own cool. My father taught my siblings and me the same thing in a different way. The worst argument for wanting to do anything that you could bring to my father was, "But Daddy, everyone else is going/doing it." His stock response was, "If everyone else jumped into the river, would that make it right for you to do the same?" (Think about the financial market crash here).

The path of mastery is to dive deep into the river of source within (don't worry, you won't drown, only the ego will be washed clean) and take the time to find your own truth, and then come from that without need of explanation or apology. When you find what's true for you and embody that, life becomes simpler, only the divine self to be pleased, only a higher wisdom guiding your judgments, no ulterior motives or agendas, only the highest good of all as a compass. There is no way to make a mistake; just abide in trust that the experience will be exactly what was needed for the outcome that needed to occur. (Think the Buddha, Mahatma Gandhi, Rosa Parks, or Martin Luther King here.)

What role would you like to play—schoolyard bully, schoolyard victim, or empowered master/radical cow? Me, I've always loved the solitary cows who would wander over to the gate to check me out and chat on those country roads of West Cork in Ireland ... without wondering what the rest of the herd must be thinking of them! They always had such kind eyes and peaceful demeanors. Radical cow suits me just fine!

Communion, Poetry of the New

A while back I read a review by Peter Howell in the *Toronto Star*[35] of a wonderful Korean movie called *Poetry*.[36] In it an older woman is diagnosed with Alzheimer's disease and decides to take a poetry class while she still can, in order to fulfill a lifelong dream of writing a poem and also to transport herself away from the terrible stresses in her everyday life. In class the teacher has the students contemplate an apple. He tells them that they've all seen the fruit thousands of times, but asks if they've ever really looked at it.

"And once it is sliced open, each and every apple reveals an interior that *no human eyes* have ever gazed upon. If you really see something, you can *feel*," the teacher says.

What an amazing awareness! What an intimate, alive experience of the newness of now without the conditioning of familiarity!

---

35 | Peter Howell, "Poetry: Seeking light, as darkness encroaches," *Toronto Star*, September 30, 2011 http://www.toronto.com/article/699760--poetry-seeking-light-as-darkness-encroaches, last accessed October 30, 2012

36 | *Poetry (Shi)*, directed by Chan-dong Lee (South Korea: UniKorea Pictures, 2010).

IN-SOURCED

I was so taken by this insight that I continued to contemplate it as I went about my day. When I served dinner to my husband that night, I shared my "aha" moment with him. I realized that the same truth applied to the baby potato I was now about to cut open with a knife. I paused in mid-slice, the magnitude of the moment moving me to stillness. This potato was giving itself to me. No one else had ever seen what I was about to see or would ever eat the nourishment that this potato was providing for me. I looked up and said to Dan, "I can't believe this potato has spent its entire life growing, just to be consumed by me. I can't bear to cut it open."

Just then a funny thing happened. My husband said, "Don't worry about it. That's why it's here. It's happy to fulfill its purpose. Go ahead and eat it."

Simultaneous to that statement I inwardly heard the potato. It was saying precisely the same thing. It was in fact quite ecstatic at the prospect of fulfilling its purpose in life and was anticipating the bliss of merging with me. I could feel it in its silent communication.

I cut it in half, gazed at it with new eyes, and put a piece in my mouth. Bliss engulfed me as I chewed and swallowed, blown away by the uniqueness of the experience and moment. I felt the energy of the food blend with my own energy. We were no longer separate and would never be again. We had merged. It was serving me selflessly. I was giving it the satisfaction of completing its purpose. The communion catapulted my awareness way beyond the physical, and my energy expanded into a state of pure ecstasy.

This is the power of focused awareness and willing participation in the newness of each moment of our lives, and it is available to all of us who have the eyes to see—whether preparing a meal or doing something as ordinary as signing our name on a credit card receipt. With awareness, it's always the *first* time: new food, new paper, new ink, new breath, new us, new now, new love.

COMMUNION, POETRY OF THE NEW

As an aside, I am reminded of how much money we are willing to spend on our love of the new and unique, the bespoke, the couture, the exotic because we seek this special feeling, which is actually ongoing as the extraordinary in the ordinary all around us all the time.

Right now we are on the cusp of a new spring—not the return of spring but a brand-new, never-before-experienced spring. As the snow drops blossom and the lilies, tulips, and peonies poke through the ground, we can be aware that we have never seen *these* blossoms before. They are new to this earth, tourists staying for a short while, getting to know us and our gardens. Will we merge with these visitors, being present to their gifts of color, texture, form, and fragrance? Will we share our gratitude for their particular and unique presence in our lives, or will we pass them by with an unconscious glance as though we've seen them many times before, hurriedly scurrying to some future moment?

Life can be the poetry of the new, the poetry of the eternally new *now*, or it can be a boring, repetitive, mundane, and unconscious experience. How blessed and powerful are we that we get to *choose* who and how we wish to be in each nanosecond of existence! Can we create ourselves to be original innocents, coming from nothing, birthed into fascination with all that is?

Jesus once said, "Verily I say unto you, except ye be converted [spiritually awakened], and become as little children [innocent and present] ye shall not enter into the kingdom of heaven [ecstasy and unification]."[37] Perhaps the poetry of the new is the gateway to heavenly realms.

The synchronicitous post script to this contemplation goes as follows: After writing this contemplation, I was looking for a book today on my shelf when I came across a book of poems by the Sufi

---

37 | Matthew Chapter 18:2-4 The Official King James Bible Online. Authorized Version (KJV). accessed October 25, 2012 *http://www.kingjamesbibleonline.org/book. php?book=Matthew&chapter=18&verse=2-4*

poet Hafiz entitled *The Subject Tonight Is Love*, translated by Daniel Ladinsky.[38] I opened it randomly, and *this* is what I found:

>
> The Vegetables
>
> Today
> The vegetables would like to be cut
> By someone who is singing God's Name.
>
> How could Hafiz know
> Such top secret information?
> Because
> Once we were all tomatoes
> Potatoes, onions or
> Zucchini.

Ah yes, indeed, the poetry of the new!

---

38 | Ladinsky, Daniel, *The Subject Tonight Is Love*. New York, New York. Penguin Compass, 2003, Page 5.

My Evening with Marilyn

Last evening I watched the movie *My Week with Marilyn*,[39] which depicts the true story of an Englishman's unexpected experience of caretaking and falling in love with Marilyn Monroe (embodied to perfection by Michelle Williams) as she filmed *The Prince and the Showgirl* in England with Sir Laurence Olivier.

Like many a movie theme, (and real-life celebrity life experience), it portrays a sensitive soul caught in the battlefield of life, struggling between following the path of the soul and the path of the ego/senses. Here before us is source, shining brightly and beautifully, as Marilyn, being fully captivated by the experience of what it is not (i.e., the human experience devoid of the awareness of itself as soul consciousness). Source, as Marilyn, identifies with the illusory stories of this particular enculturated ego/life history. She feels insecure, fragile, abandoned, and broken. She also identifies with the illusory stories mirrored back to her through the commentary of the paid staff that surrounds her—stories with such titles as "The Greatest

---

39 | *My Week with Marilyn*, directed by Simon Curtis (Beverly Hills, CA: The Weinstein Company, 2011).

Actress of Them All," "The Most Beautiful Woman," "The Greatest Sex Symbol," "The Biggest Box Office Success," "The Most Difficult to Work With," etc. What gets lost in the mix is the *essence* of the whole, authentic, complete being. Grasping at pieces of the outer shell does not give you the whole egg.

By choosing to identify with the disparate parts of one's life experience and neglecting to harmonize the whole multi-dimensional self from its denser dimensions of body, mind, and emotions to subtler dimensions of subtle, causal, and supra causal[40] (the spirit side of our awareness), one cannot hope for a holistic outcome. Identifying with fragments of who we are creates a fragmented experience of life. Furthermore, identifying with such materialistic labels creates pressure to live up to them and simultaneously fear of losing such titles. This doesn't give much opportunity to enjoy life in the present moment! For wholeness, the internal journey of the soul must progress consciously and simultaneously to the exterior experience of the life story. Conscious awareness leads to empowerment and transformation from within, which then transforms our outer life experience and our response to it.

It was touching to see the light in Marilyn Monroe flicker on and off, on and off, all the more extremely and tragically in full view of the public eye. She shone when she was *present "in the moment"* on camera experiencing the truth of the scene as she felt it.

Yet in her off times, we can identify with her lot as we struggle with our own pendulum swing between desires for wholeness, balance, love, and fulfillment and our insidious stories of fear and doubt that creep in to thwart our efforts at finding and being peace. Like her, we may experience precious moments of brightness yet struggle with following the inner voice of the soul when all around us is telling us

---

40 | For more information on this, consult Master Charles Cannon, *The Synchronicity Experience*. Nellysford, Virginia. Synchronicity Foundation International, 2002, Page 15.

we must conform to a system of society and belief that, very often, is anathema to the flow of our spirit.

On the surface, Marilyn had beauty, success, fame, an interesting career, financial stability, and the affection of three husbands and millions of fans. She was supposedly living the American dream of rags to riches, yet she was miserably unhappy and controlled by extreme stage fright, self-doubt, distrust of others, and neediness; in a world where all emotions come from a basis of either love or fear, she consistently, albeit unconsciously, chose fear. Can we relate from the material comforts of our own "North American Dream" lives?

To quell her fears and to drown the suffering voice of spirit (sadly, she had no guru to guide her), she popped pills and downed them with alcohol. From the movie it seemed as if no one saw the real essence of her or wanted her unconditionally for herself or to give full expression to herself. Everyone wanted the package, the product, delivered on time without fuss or discussion and hopefully providing the bonus of a nice profit and fame by proximity.

Although I don't know the inner workings of her mind, the late Whitney Houston comes to mind here. I heard her comment to Oprah in an interview that all she wanted to do was go away somewhere and open a fruit stand—her soul's innate desire to ground herself, perhaps, when all others saw or heard of her was that single facet known as "the voice."

Doesn't it seem as if much of the world is suffering from the same dis-ease these days? In the United States more returned veterans are dying from suicide and alcohol and drug addiction than have been killed in Afghanistan. The package/product was used up and then neglected or discarded by the powers that be, it would seem, when no longer deemed valuable. Prescription medication for anxiety and depression is the rule rather than the exception presently in North America. Psychotherapy is also common.

Marilyn was a big fan of Freud and spent many years in therapy with various doctors. Yet the mind, therapy and medication alone, while greatly helping to bring us into conceptual awareness and balance, can only take us so far. True transcendence lies beyond it. The mind is simply a data processor. Eternal wisdom comes from a much deeper place within us. But in us it most certainly is.

The French novelist Marcel Proust said, "We do not receive wisdom, we must discover it for ourselves, after a journey through the wilderness, which no one can make for us, which no one can spare us, for our wisdom is the point of view from which we must come at last to regard the world."[41]

After watching the movie, I wanted to ask her, "How can you be a light to the whole world and live your own life in darkness? How can you not be, as the Buddha said, 'A light unto your self'?"

The short answer is that while everyone turned to her to bask in her glow, she did not look sufficiently within herself and so was oblivious to its existence. She looked only to the exterior and saw its flaws. Can we relate? She therefore turned to others to prop her up. Yet no one can ever fulfill another human being for long, because the responsibility for that job rests squarely upon our own shoulders. The inner strength of connection to and respect for our own spirit is what makes us strong.

In yoga and meditation circles there is a saying: "The way out is in." Meditate. Turning inward is what we need to liberate ourselves from the bondage of history and stories, societal, religious, and personal. If we look with awareness upon all the sages in every sphere of society and in every era, we will see that they embodied wisdom and power. They did not borrow it, beg for it, or steal it. They simply *were* it. It emanated from within. They took the time and the inward journey, and they did what was necessary to drop the veils of unconscious illusion, habit, and attachment to their stories. They

---

41 | Proust, Marcel. *Remembrance of Things Past.* New York: Chelsea House, 1987

became empowered by the light and fire of the self that was always there within them (just as it is in us). They do not mean for us to lean on them. They mean to show how it is possible for us to lean on ourselves and be open to the same universal power and wisdom. We are all made of the same stuff. Only the stories differ.

We already are that. We have simply forgotten. Marilyn was so blinded by her upbringing, ongoing dramas, and self-medication that she was imbalanced to the external and forgot how to be still. Stillness is our very nature. We are all we need to be. We all have the same connections, the same divine thread, linking us to universal wisdom. It's up to us how we tune into that frequency.

Jiddu Krishnamurti said, "We all want to be famous people, and the moment we want to *be* something, we are no longer free."[42]

In the movie, Marilyn is offered the opportunity to leave it all behind and live a quiet, peaceful life in England. She refuses. Attachment to the identity we have created for ourselves can be overwhelmingly strong. Ego does not relinquish its power base easily. Yet, we create our destinies with our moment-by-moment choices throughout our lives.

An unlikely guru perhaps, she leaves us with a timely contemplation. What choices am I willing to make to create peace, bliss and freedom of spirit as **constants** in my life?

---

42 | "This Matter of Culture," Chapter 2, Jiddu Krishnamurti, J Krishnamurti Online, last accessed November 2, 2012 http://www.jkrishnamurti.org/krishnamurti-teachings/view-text.php?tid=22&chid=68518

I Am Here Now

I LAY DOWN AFTER A SITTING meditation, enjoying the bliss of pure being. I heard my inner self affirm its presence with, "I am here now."

As though I were inwardly attending a lecture, an inner guide began to parse the phrase. I listened in stillness.

"I," it said. "Who is I? Is it the physical self, the mental self, the emotional self, the cellular self? Is it the ego, the soul? Is it the flesh, the bones, the eyes, the ears? Is it the self of this moment or the moment just gone before or long ago? It's too complicated. Let's just throw I away.

"Here," it said. "Where is here? Is it here in this body, here on this bed, here in this room, this house, this city, this country, this universe, this breath, this space between the breaths? It's too complicated. Let's just throw here away.

"Now," it said. "What is now? Is now a second, a millisecond, a nanosecond? As soon as it's said, is it gone? Is it now … now … now? Have I missed it? Have I caught it? Is it gone? Now is too ephemeral and also too concrete. It's too complicated. Let's throw now away.

"What's left?" it asked. "Am. Yes. Am. Ammmmmm ... Ammmmmm ... Ammmmmm ... Ommmm ... Ommmmmm ... Ommmmm ... Aum ... Aummmm ... Aummmmmm ... A-U-M[43] ... MMMMM ..."

"Yes," it said, "Am, pure being, pure presence, am with a U for universe in the middle of it. Pure being surrounding and including the whole universe; being one with all that is; being eternal bliss. That's what you are. It's not complicated. Accept it. You are that. Creating, sustaining, destroying, creating, sustaining, destroying; Aum, am ... Thou art that."

I got it. I got it in a visceral way that I never had before. Conceptually I had been told and understood that "Aham Brahmasmai, I am Brahman,[44] Brahman is me," but this time was different. This time everything fell away, like leaves from an autumn tree. The illusion and redundancy of I and here and now was patently obvious. I willingly let them fall and dissolved into the awareness of the eternal "Am," vibrating, ecstatic, complete being.

Yes! Am is what I am! And so it is with you! Amen and Ameen to that.

---

[43] | "The Sanskrit letter Om consists of A, U, and M. With 'A' one opens the throat, with 'M' one closes the lips. 'U' denotes all that is between the opening and closing of the operation of sound in the human sound box. Om thus denotes the production of all names of which a human being is capable. Therefore, it is chosen as the symbol of the Supreme Self who is all that exists." – Swami Jyotirmayananda, *Concentration and Meditation*, Miami, Florida, Published by Swami Lalitananda, 1971. Page 53. See Resources.

[44] | "Pranava (Om) is the bow, The individual soul is the arrow, Brahman or the Absolute is the target, O Aspirant, hit the target, with persistent vigilance; And just as the arrow becomes one with the target, So too become merged in Brahman (the Absolute)." – Mundaka Upanishad - Swami Jyotirmayananda, *Concentration and Meditation*, Miami, Florida, Published by Swami Lalitananda, 1971. Page 53. See Resources.

Do You Know Where You're Going?

Remember that old Diana Ross song? *"Do you know where you're going to? Do you like the things that life is showing you? Where are you going to? Do you know?"*

Well, I had another "aha" moment this morning returning from the airport after dropping my husband off for his flight. As I navigated my way out of Pearson International, I remembered how in the past the prospect of driving to and from the airport terrified me! All those roads and signs combined with driving at speed in heavy traffic overwhelmed my mind, and anxiety ensued. Which way do I go? What route do I need to take? 409? 427? East, west, north, south? Do I need to switch lanes? Have I got enough time to switch over before the exit? What if I get it wrong? Where would I end up, hopelessly lost, never to find my way home again? Aghhh! Such is the process of fear-based thinking.

I recalled this as I kept my eye on the 427 signs ... 427 West, 427 North ... I was on my way, then 407 exit, turning onto 407 East to Markham Road ... Smooth sailing all the way home. How easy and enjoyable was that! The light bulb went on. It was only painful when I

IN-SOURCED

wasn't sure *where* I was going and even less sure *how* to get there. Once I knew exactly where I wanted to end up, did the necessary work to find out how to get there, knew what to look for along the way, and disregarded all the other signs and distractions, the process was easy, smooth, and enjoyable.

What a metaphor for our lives. If we know where we want to end up—and I don't mean what job, house, neighborhood or income bracket, marital partner, number of kids, etc., I mean if we know where we *ultimately want to end up*, and for me that would be in a *constant state of peace, joy, love, and fulfillment to the fullest extent possible ... a unified state of existence*—that's a huge problem out of the way right there. I don't have to be dazzled and confused by every other path, bauble, and distraction along the way that might take me elsewhere and get me diverted off route, interesting or torturous, dead-end or scenic though the alternate roads might be. (Ultimately all roads lead here, so it's really a matter of how conscious, smooth, and expeditious we intend our trip to be.)

Once I know where I want to end up, I simply figure out the most effective route, seek the advice of those who have mastered the journey and are familiar with the destination, and look for the sign posts along the way that let me know I'm headed in the right direction. What might those signs say? Let's have some fun with this:

- Highway ETR: Express Tranquility Route

- Highway 427 North: 4 you 2 be in 7th Heaven, led by the North Star of your soul's GPS

- Highway 404:   4 Optimism 4 all

- Highway 401:   4 Our Oneness

Then, if I am experiencing the reverse of where I want to be I know I'm headed off course (Fear-Based Road; Despair Alley;

Isolation Highway; Revenge Route 666; Material Myth Blvd.; Signs announcing the towns of Stress, Anger, and Resistance).

All is not lost. I simply take the next exit and resume the journey. I keep looking for signs that I'm getting closer to where I choose to be. How do the motorists look who are traveling alongside me (the company I keep)? Are they uplifting, encouraging, and peaceful? Do they help when I need guidance on my way? Or are they honking at me, too busy texting, intoxicated, or generous with the middle finger? Is the scenery uplifting or dragging me down (where I work, live, socialize, my thoughts, emotions, and words)? Do I need to pull over and take stock of where I'm *really* headed if I keep going in this direction?

When we know what our ultimate destination is, informed ourselves of the best way to get there, and are on that road, then we can forget the destination completely and enjoy the journey itself, secure in the knowledge that we have nothing to worry about. The course is set. We are doing and being all we can to get there. Our vehicle (the body) is properly serviced (proper exercise and meditation). There is premium gas in our tank (healthy diet and positive thinking). We are wakeful behind the wheel and aware of the signs that we are getting closer to home. Whatever happens now is appropriate as we are secure in the knowing that this is the appropriate road for us. Fear drops away.

We feel happiness and peace within. In that very moment, such blissful awareness becomes the destination in itself. We feel as fulfilled and relaxed as if we were already there, and to our great surprise, we find that in this state of peace and bliss, home is wherever we happen to be.

We discover, to our great delight, that the way is the destination and the destination is the way. We know where we are going, and we are already there/here!

Bon voyage on your journey from here to here!

The Fog and the Sun

The dawn rose on a beautiful day. Fog blanketed the ravine, rising off the river and hanging from the trees, looking mystical and ghostly. Visibility was limited as I made my way down the path from my home to the yoga studio to teach class.

By the end of class, the sun had risen higher and warmed to the task of dispersing the fog. The higher it got, the hotter it got. The hotter it got, the more the fog disappeared, as though it had never been. The ravine and river were revealed in all their delightful, sparkling glory.

What a perfect metaphorical lesson, source. Thank you for teaching me once again without saying a word.

Think of the fog as the stories we surround ourselves with. The thicker the fog, the harder it is to see through. If we can't see anything else, then this *must* be real; the fog is all there is, and there's nothing we can do about it, right?

"It's not my fault there's this thick fog in my life. It's not my fault I can't move this way or that. It's the fog's fault. Just look at how thick and heavy it is. Life is hard and dull. Life is full of oppression. Don't take my word for it. Just look at the fog! That's all there is. We might as well resign ourselves to the fact. It's never going to change. I can't forgive it for being so foggy. I am bitter, angry, and full of despair, but that's how it is. I lash out at the fog. I beat it with a stick until I am exhausted with the effort, but it will not leave me alone. It's an awful, terrible villain, a cruel bully, and I am powerless in its grasp! Woe is me. This is my depressing destiny in life."

But then the sun comes along. The sun represents the guru or spiritual teachings of universal truth. A glimmer of light appears through the dreariness. What's this? You begin to make out shapes through the veil.

"Are those tree branches? Hush. Was that a squirrel scurrying up the trunk? No, it can't be. There is only fog. Always has been, always will be ..."

Now you're starting to feel the heat. Soft greens and dark browns are mottling the opaqueness. Come to think of it, it's not so opaque anymore.

"What's happening here? I'm not sure I like this. Where's the fog going? It's all I've ever known. I was comfortable here. I had nowhere to go and nothing to do. I had no responsibility for my life. I could just sit here and blame the fog for my experience."

The sun is high. The fog is gone. Your vision is clear. You can see things about yourself and others that you never saw before. It's unfamiliar and uncomfortable but enlightening. Others can see things about you that were hidden from both of you in the fog.

"Oh God, I don't like this. I feel naked. I feel exposed. I feel embarrassed and ashamed that people will see I'm human, with all the imperfections that go along with that. (I have not yet come to the realization that everyone else is human and perfectly imperfect also.) No. I will not be made wrong or ordinary or fallible or vulnerable. It's the sun's fault. Just look at how bright and hot it is. It's oppressive. It's a bully. Why doesn't it go away and give me back my fog? I was happy with my fog. I can't forgive it for being so sunny. What's it trying to prove? I beat the light with a stick, but it will not leave me alone. I am exhausted with the effort. I am powerless in its grasp! Woe is me. I hate the sun. The sun has ruined my life! It will not allow me to dwell in the twilight and the darkness. I'm not ready for the lessons the sun is bringing to my attention. I'm not ready to take responsibility for how I choose to live and love and be. It's a bad sun. I will lock myself indoors, close the blinds, and pretend it doesn't exist and that none of this ever happened. I will create my own fog and happily despise it for the rest of my life!

This much I learned from the sun. Now I have a choice: the fog or the light. Until I am ready to stand a naked warrior in the light, I will hide in the darkness and tell everyone I know how the sun is to blame for my plight!"

This is sometimes the way of the spiritual path. Every spiritual teacher who stands unflinchingly in the light of truth incurs the wrath of disgruntled, wounded egos from time to time. (Jesus come to mind for anyone?) The sun shines to show the magnificence of all existence, exactly as it is, yet the ego sees only the shortcomings and blames it on the light. The guru says the only thing harder to find than an authentic master is an authentic student![45]

Such is the way of the processing ego! It's all appropriate. The sun is benign and takes nothing personally. It is there for those who treasure it and for those who despise it alike. Its duty is to shine. We get to choose whether to block it out or revel in it. And sometimes we have to do one before we are ready to do the other. Evolution evolves anyway.

But why settle for the booby prize when you are being handed the winning lottery ticket of self-realization? Why not make the sun your friend and turn golden in the process?

---

45 | Master Charles Cannon.

IN-SOURCED

(I offer this story with gratitude to the feet of my spiritual teachers whose stories, teachings, and transmissions, along with the sun and the fog, inspired this contemplation. Jai Gurudevas!)

I Am No-Body, I Am Soul

When I visited Varanasi, India's holiest city, I had the privilege of meeting Sri Satua Baba at his ashram on the banks of the Ganges, situated right behind the burning *ghats*. He is a very aged yet youthful and enlightening being, with a twinkle in his eye and a gentleness and generosity of presence. He hosted my guru, Master Charles Cannon, and his monks while my daughter and I (and others) stayed at a guest house a short walk away. We attended daily to spend time with them.

On one occasion, Swamiji had us all take boat rides across the Ganges to the other, more pastoral side, where the ashram had a farm. After disembarking, we walked across the long, sandy dunes until we reached a fertile, quiet oasis that felt like a completely different world from the ancient, heavily populated buildings just a riverbank away. We spent a delightful and unforgettable afternoon in the company of two enlightening masters, touring the simple dwellings and admiring the lush vegetable plantings and immaculate sacred cows, including Swamiji's favorite, Krishna.

Swamiji and his monks, along with Master Charles and his monks, led the way back to the boats in the setting sun. The procession of serene form and renunciant colored robes of orange and white set against the backdrop of the beautifully illuminated ancient city, whose golden lights were reflected in the holy river, was simply too exquisite a scene to commit only to memory. I wanted to capture the moment on my camera. I asked my daughter to do the same with hers. However, try as we might, our attempts to photograph the scene yielded indistinct, abstract, watercolor-type renderings, reminiscent of an Impressionist painting. They looked really beautiful but were very blurry. Hmmm, what was going on here?

We gathered on the marble floor outside the ashram buildings on our return. Master Charles (MC) and Swamiji sat in white plastic garden chairs. We sat cross-legged at their feet, listening to the holy chanting of evening *aarti* being performed by the priests below us at water's edge. Fragrant smoke drifted in from the funeral pyres on the ghats. Paper kites flew in the twilight sky, and an owl glided overhead and landed on a peak. Sri Satua Baba offered us delectably sweet Indian treats from his own hand—food for the body and the soul. The two gurus occasionally conversed with each other or with us before drifting back into a blissful silence.

After some time spent in this idyllic state, content to watch the ashram cat pad her way quietly under MC's seat and curl up at his feet, and wondering at my most excellent good fortune to be in this place at this time with these people and being able to share it all with my daughter Robyn, Carol, a member of our party turned to me and asked if I would take her picture with the two gurus.

I said, "Maybe you should ask their permission first. The images we took on the dunes are blurred."

So, up she went, and she asked if they would agree to have their photo taken with her. As if Swamiji had been privy to our conversation, he looked over at us photographers and said, with his limited English, "It's good that you ask. I am no-body. I am soul. You take picture without ask, I am no-body, so no in picture."

His identity is so dissolved in absolute consciousness, in oneness, that unless he calls it back into his body, he won't show up clearly to the camera's lens.

I had read of another Indian sage, Lahiri Mahasaya, the guru of Paramahansa Yogananda's guru (Swami Sri Yukteshwar), who only ever appeared in the one photo that he agreed to have taken. Others who tried to capture him on film were left with a blank shot.[46]

Now I know this sounds pretty strange to those of us confined to the denser dimensions of body, mind, and emotions, but isn't it nice to know there are those among us who are a little further along the road who can be a tangible example as to what's possible for all of mankind?

I am no-body. I am soul. How liberating it must be to be able to leave the cage of the body at will and dance among the heavens, at peace and at one with all, and yet to have the power to return as required! No wonder he looks so youthful for his ninety-something years! People pay a lot to travel to space in a specially constructed and very confining rocket. This enlightening sage does it freely and for free. Sign me up! I'll have what he's having! I am no-body. I am soul.

---

46 | Yogananda, Paramahansa. *Autobiography of a Yogi*. Los Angeles, CA: Self-Realization Fellowship, 1998. Pages 11 and 343. "I am Spirit. Can your camera reflect the omnipresent Invisible?" – Lahiri Mahasaya

Spiders and Webs

Back in 2005 I stayed at Synchronicity Sanctuary for Modern Spirituality in the Blue Ridge Mountains of Virginia to train to be a Synchronicity contemporary meditation teacher. To be exact, I stayed at the hermitage guest quarters, which necessitated a good fifteen- to twenty-minute hike through the forest several times a day to get to the classroom and dining quarters of the sanctuary itself.

The adventure of that hike—up the hill, through the treed and leaf-carpeted pathway, across the wooden bridge overlooking a vast ravine, up the wooden steps, down the paved roadway, onto the gravel path, and into the building used for our intimate gathering of prospective teachers—was a meditation in itself. Every day was different as spring opened itself up gently, moment by moment, greening and blossoming with delicate dogwoods and sturdy oaks. The forest was an un-credited teacher on the curriculum, the walk itself, a most enlightening free period. I felt so blessed that such a place existed and (selfishly) that so few people seemed to be aware of it! I luxuriated in the solitude and the company of nature. To this day I still regard certain trees there as my special friends. It's a nice fantasy that I feel sure must be shared by others who have walked the same path!

Training to be a meditation teacher is not like training to be a mechanic or a computer engineer, where you learn a set of skills that are external to yourself and then apply them in the world in order to earn a living. Those kinds of skills may not affect you in any internal way other than through the accrual of information and illusory self-esteem. In meditation teacher training, there is an external skill set, but along with this goes the internal transformational course, which burrows through the layers of data to the essence of who we are and begins clearing out the ignorance and stories that make up our lives thus far and that we unknowingly assume are all that is. We are encouraged to move from the dense dimensions of body, mind, and emotions to the subtle experience of who we *truly* are. It's quite the ride to let go of all we've ever assumed was reality and open up to new possibilities. It's all we've ever known. What else could there possibly be? But we must, as Charles Du Bos said, "Be ready at any moment to sacrifice what we are for what we could become."[47]

On the second-to-last morning of the course, I awoke to find it had rained very lightly overnight. I had risen a little later than usual, being tired from the late hours and the intensity of the experience, and began to hurry up the hill to the forest to make my way to morning meditation on time. Because of my hurry, I was less wakeful than usual—that is, until I was completely stopped in my tracks by the sight that awaited me as I entered the forest. The entire forest floor seemed to be woven with diamonds and pearls. It sparkled in the morning light that filtered through the trees. What had previously been a dun-colored canvas was now glistening and glittering. On close inspection, I noticed that the entire leafy ground was covered in spider webs. The webs were coated by raindrops that outlined

---

47 | Du Bos, Charles, *Approximations*. Paris: Plon Nourrit et Cie, 1922.

their beautiful, delicate forms. How stunning! How otherworldly and magical!

The light bulb of awareness went on. So this is what Alan Scherr, our teacher, was trying to explain to us. The simple fact was that these spider webs were there all the time, but they were *so subtle* that they were invisible to me. I had been surrounded by these every day, but I had not been aware of them. If you had told me about them, I would have seriously doubted their existence, and most likely you too, for even suggesting such a possibility. What a masterful spiritual lesson.

In just such a way, we are surrounded by subtle dimensions of ever-increasing fineness and light. Yet if we do not have the eyes to see, we are blind to the experience. We ourselves are made of fineness and light, yet in our unconsciousness, we say "What are you talking about? I don't see anything, and therefore I don't believe you. One of us is crazy, and I don't think it's me!"

It's all appropriate. We do not see until we see. And when we see, no one can make us not see. We change on a fundamental level of being. Our programming is updated, and we evolve to a finer, more enlightened version of ourselves. What was once dun and dense begins to sparkle and glisten. So be it, and so it is.

I would like to thank spiders everywhere for teaching us that from seemingly dense creatures the most delicate creations can emerge. Yes!

Identity Loss and Reward

Have you ever wondered about your identity? Who are you, really? What is an identity anyway?

I looked up the meaning on Dictionary.com. There are five meanings given, which is interesting in itself, if you think about it. Here are four of them:

1. The *condition* of being oneself or itself, and not another: *He doubted his own identity.*

2. Condition or *character* as to who a person or what a thing is: *a case of mistaken identity.*

3. The *state* or fact of being the same one as described.

4. The *sense* of self, providing sameness and continuity in personality over time and sometimes disturbed in mental illnesses, as schizophrenia.[48]

---

48 | *Dictionary.com*, s.v. "identity," last accessed October 12, 2012, http://dictionary.reference.com/browse/identity?s=t.

IN-SOURCED

It sounds rather vague and transitory, doesn't it—a condition, a character, a state, a sense? And yet, we *cling to it* with great ferocity.

Here's the thing that fascinates me: We think the identity is who we are, our very essence, yet if you look at the definitions and at how I described our relationship with it, you will notice that it is not who we are at all. It is an appendage. It is something separate that we can identify with, that describes us, that we can doubt, and that can change according to our mental, emotional, and physical health and outlook.

Our identity is something we build over time. We work hard to accrue characteristics that we project as who we are, and then we totally buy into the story we have crafted so painstakingly. But if this is who we are, then who were we before we developed such characteristics and stories? And who will we be if and when they change?

This contemplation came to focus recently as my health and vitality took a downward turn. A medical test showed the possibility that I had a serious health issue. Hanging out in hospitals to investigate further didn't sit well with me. Sitting in waiting areas among obviously and not-so-obviously unwell people brought up resistance for me.

"I'm not one of these people," prattled my identity to itself. "I'm healthy, fit, and strong. I shouldn't be here. There must have been a mistake in the test." I told myself this despite obvious symptoms that suggested otherwise! How funny is that! Who said that anyway—the body, the mind, the emotions, the ego, the self? Talk about a crowded house!

So anyway, as I sat in meditation this morning, I had a vision of an ice cube, all hard, rigid, and square, being placed in a large bowl of water. I saw the hard edges soften as the ice began to melt. Slowly the ice cube that was so defined and separate became amorphous and ever smaller. Finally it was completely dissolved.

IDENTITY LOSS AND REWARD

This was my metaphysical lesson on identity. The ice cube represented the individual identity and the bowl of water the ocean of consciousness. The identity is all hard-edged and isolated in its egotistical self-consciousness. "I am this. I am not that." It clings to its qualities of separateness and defends its position to remain that way. It fears losing what defines it. But when it is placed in the vast ocean of consciousness, it begins to melt. It appears to lose its distinguishing features.

But where did they go? What is lost? Every part of it melts into and merges with this ocean. Nothing whatsoever is lost, but instead what used to be the inflexible cube now through fluidity gains access to the whole of the ocean of existence. It is one with all that is. Individuation becomes wholeness through unification. Limited awareness is traded in for universal consciousness.

So that which I thought was special and worth preserving at all costs was merely a hologram I built around my essence. A prison of my own making; a prison I got so used to living in that I mistook it for me. But when I let go—*just let go*—I still get to be all I ever was, without any loss at all, and I am simultaneously so much more.

And to me, that is a pretty good reward for losing my identity!

Just Another Day in Paradise

Yesterday I sent out an e-mail announcement to all my students that I was taking a break from teaching for an indefinite period of time. It was another hammer strike upon the structure of my self-identity. Last week I faced health issues. This week I faced walking away from something that had been an integral part of my life for the last fifteen years.

From the superficial problem of how to respond to the question of, "Do you work outside the home?"; to the deeper experience of community, mutual love, and respect that had built up between myself and my students; to the awareness that I provided a gathering spot for like minds to share, support, and educate each other on all matters of holistic health and conscious awareness that I was for now, at least, closing the door on—these were all major considerations and attachments. These students were much more to me than students. We were group souls walking the *camino* of enlightenment together, nudging each other along as required.

And with one announcement, I had brought an end to it all, it seemed. Some of the students were sad. Some were grateful and sad.

Some were proactive with questions about who to learn from next. Some were silent. Some took it in stride.

You might wonder if I questioned my sanity.

"What have you done?"

In truth, I had previewed the scenario many times prior to making this decision and decided against doing it for fear of upsetting others. I also feared upsetting myself because I loved these people and was attached to their company. But this time was different. As the old saying goes, "We have nothing to fear but fear itself."

My guru taught me well about peace of mind being the God within. All decisions need to be made with this in mind. There are not enough riches on the planet to compensate for a lack of peace of mind. Though all of the above facts were positive aspects of my life experience, I noticed a diminishment in my peace of mind. Something was prompting me incessantly from within. "Now," it said. "It's time. Do it now!" And as a result, I couldn't completely relax. I wasn't sleeping well. It was popping up in the stillness of my meditations.

I would argue with this guidance, rationalizing, "This is my *seva* (spiritual service). I am blessed with a stress-free job in a beautiful environment. I have great students and work just enough hours, and we uplift each other. I have the summers off to pursue my own interests. I get to do yoga and meditate and am even paid for the privilege. I have a chance to share universal wisdom with people who are *actually and sincerely interested*! How rare is that? Why should I stop?"

I thought it was a pretty convincing argument, so I didn't take action. It wasn't *logical*. It didn't make *sense!* Really, source, what *are* you thinking?

But source doesn't shine a light way up the road for us to see what's coming. It expects us to trust that it sees the big picture and is looking after everything up ahead so we don't have to. We just have to trust, without all the details that so comfort us. Trust and take action in the now.

And so today, I stood in front of my last class for now. We enjoyed our time together and hugged our good-byes in the bittersweet moment that was filled with new possibilities for each of us. My heart was filled with gratitude for the blessings of these lovely people in my life.

After class, I stepped outside the studio into the sunshine. The birds were singing a delightful chorus. The plum trees were more laden with blossoms than I could ever remember. Daffodils and purple hyacinths danced and perfumed the breeze respectively. A few red admiral butterflies flitted about the garden. No matter what went before or what may come after, today was just another day in paradise. Peace of mind enabled me to savor it all.

The Liberation of Loss

As I have already mentioned, thus far in my life, I've had to let go of a lot of things I *thought* I needed for my personal well-being, peace of mind, and happiness, just as, most likely, many of you also have. We all get the lessons we need to grow from.

To name a few of my losses: my homeland; my parents and relatives too numerous to mention; family home; siblings; nanny; childhood family pets; jobs; friends; colleagues; first love; financial security; culture; social standing; illusions about a perfect life and marriage; miscarriage; youthful beauty; faithful family dog; my children as they grew up and moved out; gurus; my health (temporarily many times); dear ones suddenly and violently; livelihood; identification with livelihood; illusion of living in a safe, stable, sane world; illusion of being completely fulfilled by another; and more than once, nearly my life.

You get the idea. You may also identify with some or many of the above. With each loss there has been grief and some anxiety about how life would go on and how it would feel without these experiences in my life that I had thoughtlessly assumed would be constants. In the natural grieving process, there was a clinging to the past and a fear of going alone into the unknown future.

Sometimes when we are stuck in the darkness of each new sadness and fear, the truth of life that unfolded with each previous loss is temporarily forgotten. It's a curious phenomenon where the dazzling lights of the drama blind us to the also dazzling lights of universal truth.

For here is the truth that I have discovered with each loss: What is actually lost is the fixation upon attachment—the illusion that we need to plug our awareness into other persons, places, and things to be complete when nothing could be further from the truth! As we begin to gain distance from and perspective over that which we think we have lost, two pearls of wisdom become evident.

First, life goes on, and we are actually made stronger, not weaker, by the disconnection. We are more liberated by the realization that we can still be whole with less.

Second, nothing is ever truly lost. It just transforms from a dense experience to a more subtle one, a bit like moving all your CDs onto your MP3 player and then giving away all the hard copies.

In this case, the hard copy is the physical manifestation of people, places, and things, and your MP3 player is your internal hard drive of heart and mind. We may not be able to reach out and touch it, but if the right button is pressed, there it is—supremely portable within our inner awareness and not just in memory form. As we acquire the ability to really tune into the stillness and listen, we can hear the universe whispering the experience of the eternal now and the eternal existence of all forms of itself.

"There is no loss," it tells us. "There is no need to attach ourselves to person, place, thing or story. We are all dancing particles of the same source material shifting like kaleidoscopic forms of the same one essence."

In time, with each loss we gain more—more freedom, more awareness of eternity, more lightness of being—and all that's really lost is the story that's kept us earthbound and stagnating in our illusions about how life should be.

Whatever comes, let it come. Whatever goes, let it go. It's all a temporary and yet eternal dance.

Just Be

What I thought were sufferings were jewels.
What I thought were sharp edges were caressing nudges.
What I thought was abandonment was compassionate nurturing.
What I thought was the enemy was the teacher.
What I thought was ignorance was the lesson.
What I thought was darkness was you holding the light.
What I thought was death was eternal light.
What I thought was the other was you.
What I thought was you was my own self.

"Don't think," says the self.
"Just be."

House Beautiful

> If you would be loved, be loving.
> —Master Charles Cannon

I wrestled with my husband to let me take over some of the outdoor garden chores this summer. He is an avid gardener who loves to work, and being outside in nature is a balancing tool for all those hours spent indoors at an office desk or stuck in traffic. But there is a lot of upkeep and maintenance required on our home—fences to be painted, hedges to be trimmed, grass to be cut and edged, flowers to be dead-headed, the driveway and flower beds to be weeded, the pool to be cleaned, and the cars to be washed. I'm not complaining. I'm grateful for the abundance that necessitates such chores and for having the home of our dreams.

So, against his protestations that he could do it all, I took over the grass cutting (he agreed to trim the edges—deal), the pool cleaning, and the weeding of the driveway. It's all very meditative, and the outdoor physical exertion is wonderfully grounding and integrating for mind and body.

My mind processed as I worked. It just makes sense to take good care of the house and garden that takes care of you, right? It's an expensive investment, and it only makes sense to manage one's initial investment wakefully in order to reap the benefits of enjoyment in the present moment while ensuring the prospects of maximum return on investment when the time comes to sell and move on, God/source/the universe willing.

But more importantly, I also believe that what you pour love into will be a container filled with love, an expression of love (and thus expressing the vibration of love) ultimately, so everyone/thing wins. I have also viewed our home, which we have renovated extensively, as an extension of our own energetic vibration, feeling that we have grown and matured as it has (or vice versa). Do you think it's possible to tell a lot about the state of a person by stepping inside his or her home? How does it look? How does it make you feel?

I've noticed that people who hoard things frequently tend to have financial woes. They are often negative and fear-based (thus the hoarding), not trusting a benevolent universe to provide as needed and not realizing that they are not allowing any space for universal energy to flow and co-create with them.

A chaotic home makes for a chaotic mind, the former being a mirror of the latter; this was my own experience before I got into yoga and meditation!

What does your home say to and about you? Are you listening to what it's trying to tell you?

Remember, your home is your friend. It provides you with shelter and comfort and is there for you at the end of a long day with the welcome mat out, ready and waiting. It also serves your needs as you prepare to begin a new day, unless you stifle the life out of it through indifference, ignorance, and neglect.

Does your home bear a striking resemblance to other friends (or enemies) in your life? Is it mirroring something in you that is calling for your care and attention?

Your car could be viewed in the same light of friendship or neglect. If you love and respect it, it serves you well. Neglect it and it may drop you as a friend and leave you stranded!

Now let's take this topic one step further. After cutting the grass last week, I came in to take a shower. As I shaved my legs, I realized that, in that moment, I was looking after another house and garden—mowing the "lawn" on my legs, washing the "car" on my head, plucking the "weeds" in my brows. Then I had to paint the face and nourish the skin with cream as I might paint the fence and nourish the flowers with plant food and water, dead-heading the withered blossoms as I manicured my nails.

Furthermore, just as my car needs to be taken out for a drive regularly to keep it operating smoothly, my body too requires daily exercise. As my car needs clean fuel to perform optimally, so does my body need clean, simple nutrition and my mind a nurturing meditation, positive focus and adequate rest to keep the lines clean and the gears shifting smoothly.

Could it be that that's all we really have to do in life? Live clean, live simple. Take care of what we *have* control over. Prioritize a healthy respect for this house and garden and vehicle that will accompany us from cradle to grave. Maximize our investment so that when the time comes to cash in our chips, the journey will have been as balanced, whole, and utterly alive as we have the power to make it as we wakefully, consciously tend our bodily home of the spirit to the best of our ability, no matter how many times we move houses or change our four-wheeled vehicles.

Many of us seek to change the world purely through an external focus. We say, "Let's fix the problem with that person over there or that neighborhood, race, or nation. Then life will be beautiful and I will be happy."

If everyone is focused "over there," it stands to reason that no one is paying attention to their own plots. Take a look around at all the obese, neglected bodies—at all the messed-up minds and broken hearts. It's not hard to discern that the external focus is just not working to bring harmony to society and lasting contentment and fulfillment personally and universally.

Imagine a better world where all we have to do is take proper care of ourselves, each person being fully responsible for one thing: oneself. Start there. Love, honor, cherish, and respect yourself, your higher noble self, your house and garden of the soul. Make sure your home is built on a foundation of integrity to withstand life's storms. Be a love affair unto yourself. Fall in love with the only companion you will have for sure, for life: your sacred life force! Give yourself the friendship and love first that you seek in the other, and from that point of fulfillment, allow friendship and love to flow to others.

Take the time in meditation to tune into the reality of who you are beyond what you've been told by others. Be your own loving parent, and allow yourself to flourish. (Let's face it, the perfect parent probably doesn't exist because we're all on a learning curve and dealing with our individual issues, but we can *choose* to support ourselves in the way we may have wished that our parents had. The perfect parent resides within, ready to be awakened and called to service!) I'll say it again: *allow yourself to flourish instead of poking at your perceived flaws!* Be the role model you wish you'd had.

Just as an eye for an eye makes the whole world blind, wakeful respect for the self makes the whole world vibrate with self-respect and love. Imagine the cumulative effect of such a society; I can almost hear Louis Armstrong sing, "What a wonderful world!"

What one step do you think you could take to make your house beautiful in this moment?

Afterword

As I mentioned in a previous contemplation, Maura Radford, the woman who worked as our nanny and housekeeper for thirty-five years, and who lives in Ireland, turned ninety this year. Her health took a downturn this week, and though she has rallied for now, my siblings and I were talking about what she has meant to us. We all used the same word to describe what she gave us and how we felt about her: *love*.

She never married. She lived with her sister, who pre-deceased her. She never made a lot of money, lived in a big house, or drove a fancy car (or any car, for that matter). She never wielded force over her seven charges, unruly though a house full of kids might be. Her power was love. She really loved us and cared for us as though we were her very own children. She was gentle. She was kind. We loved her so much that we would do anything for her, even to this day.

I asked my friend, Jai Krishnanand, a homeopath and practitioner of radiesthesia, which encompasses long distance energy healing, to check on her this week when she was very weak. Though he knew very little about her and was checking her from thousands of miles away, his comment to me afterward was, "What sweet energy she has."

To be ready to leave the body at the end of our lifetime still sweet and surrounded by and remembered for love is a wonderful accomplishment. It is an accomplishment that is achieved moment by moment according to the choices we make right here and now and not something we can decide at the last minute, never knowing when that minute will be.

To repeat Master Charles's quotation: "Life is simple. Minds make it complex."

When we choose love we get to enjoy it in life, leave its vibration behind with our loved ones *and* merge with it when we relinquish the body in death. Now that's living according to our true source-full nature!

Love, it's such a nice afterword.

About the Author

Founder of Ah Yogahh Sanctuary, for fifteen years HELEN CONNOLLY has taught yoga and meditation. She is an accredited Integral® Yoga instructor and Synchronicity Contemporary Meditation teacher. Born in Ireland, she is the mother of two grown children and lives an everyday miraculous life with her husband in Markham, Ontario, Canada.

Resources

I have not included how-to instructions for meditation in this book. Instead I provide you, in no particular order, with the resources that benefited me, so that you may explore for yourself what feels appropriate for you. The logo of Integral® Yoga states, "Truth is One, Paths are Many." See if any of these paths resonate with you. If you have any questions you may reach me at:

helen.connolly@ahyogahh.com
or through my website www.ahyogahh.com.

Christina Thomas-Fraser:
www.innerlightinstitute.com

Sri Swami Satchidananda
Integral® Yoga:
http://www.yogaville.org/

Master Charles Cannon
Synchronicity Foundation for Modern Spirituality:
www.synchronicity.org

Jai Krishnanand:
Jaimangal (Jai) Krishnanand is a homeopath specializing in radiesthesia (vibrational energy healing), holistic nutrition and iridology, practicing in Burnaby, British Columbia, Canada. He may be reached for consultation at jaimangalk@gmail.com

Suresh Goswamy:
Suresh Goswamy is the founder of Yoga and Meditation Studios of Canada. He may be reached at sgoswamy@rogers.com

Blaine Watson:
Blaine Watson is a Vedic Astrologer, located in Oliver, British Columbia, Canada. He may be reached for consultation at blainepw@gmail.com

Kia Scherr:
Kia Scherr is co-founder of One Life Alliance, created in response to the 26/11 terrorist attack in Mumbai that took the lives of her husband and daughter, Alan and Naomi Scherr.
She can be reached at Kia@onelifealliance.org

Paramahansa Yogananda
Self-Realization Fellowship:
http://www.yogananda-srf.org/

Swami Jyotirmayananda
Yoga Research Foundation:
http://www.yrf.org/

Osho:
www.osho.com

Sri Sathya Sai Baba:
http://www.sathyasai.org/